D1562220

MARRIAGE, DIVORCE AND ASTROLOGY

Also by Teri King:

Love, Sex and Astrology
Business, Success and Astrology
The Astrologer's Diet Book

MARRIAGE
DIVORCE
&
ASTROLOGY

by
Teri King

BARNES & NOBLE BOOKS
A DIVISION OF HARPER & ROW, PUBLISHERS
New York, Cambridge, Philadelphia, San Francisco
London, Mexico City, São Paulo, Sydney

First published in Great Britain in 1982 by Allison and Busby Limited. It is here reprinted by arrangement.

First BARNES & NOBLE BOOKS edition published 1984.

Library of Congress Cataloging in Publication Data

King, Teri.
    Marriage, divorce, and astrology.

    Originally published: London : Allison & Busby, 1982.
    1. Astrology and marriage. 2. Astrology and divorce. I Title.
BF1729.L6K56 1984   133.5'864677   83-48968
ISBN 0-06-464086-8 (pbk.)

84 85 86 87 88   10 9 8 7 6 5 4 3 2 1

CONTENTS

I should like to dedicate this book
to astrology — which has never let me down —
and to my husband Ken, about whom I can
honestly say the same. And lastly to you,
dear reader, whether you be married,
single, divorced or simply desperate.

INTRODUCTION

ASTROLOGY is a complex science which has of necessity been treated in a general way in this book. I should, however, like to discuss briefly the mechanics of the subject in the hope of correcting any misconceptions that the reader may start with.

The cynic will usually ask: "How can a forecast for any Zodiac sign be accurate for everyone born under it?" The obvious answer is, of course, that all horoscopes must be general unless the astrologer is able to work from specific details about the hour, date and year of birth of the individual in question. As an example, let us take a person born on 3 September. Broadly speaking he or she is the subject of Virgo, a Virgoan, for the Sun occupies that section of the sky known as Virgo between August 23 and September 23. We must also, however, account for the position of the Moon, which enters a fresh sign approximately every forty-eight hours. It may have occupied Gemini on the day in question and in this instance our subject would become Virgoan-Geminian. (Here it must be explained that some characteristics from the Moon will work at the subconscious level, so our particular case will have the will-power of a Virgoan but with Gemini influencing their subconscious.)

Progressing further, we must consider the sign rising at the exact time of birth. It is an ever-changing process as it takes approximately two hours for each sign to pass over the horizon. It may be that Virgo was ascending on the hour in question, in which case the image presented to the world — the personality — will again be Virgoan, thus making our example a Virgoan-Geminian-Virgoan. This procedure is carried on through all the nine planets, each depicting a feature of the subject's make-up: the position, the signs they occupy and the aspects formed from one another all play an important part.

If we return to our example we will notice that two of the three important characteristics are in Virgo, and so our subject will be a typical Virgoan. If on the other hand the Sun were to have been in Virgo, with the Moon and ascendant both in Gemini, then he would display all the traits associated with a true Geminian, despite a probable belief to the contrary.

Astrology can be used to assess·any aspect of life and within the ensuing pages it examines close personal relationships and attempts to answer questions such as the following:

Should the independent Aquarian seriously consider marriage?

What is likely to send your average Geminian screaming to the divorce court?

Is it really the end of the world when a Cancerian marriage breaks down? And if not, how do you begin to pick up the pieces?

What about the children of broken marriages or liaisons — how should you help them to adjust to life without a parent or to accept a new one?

For each sign there are several sections that describe: your typical general characteristics; how marriage is likely to affect you; your potential as a husband or as a wife; what sort of ex-spouse you might make; how you would take to a communal life-style; whether cohabitation would suit you; how you rate as a lover; how well children of each sign are likely to cope with divorce, or adapt to remarriage; and finally, given all the preceding information, what sort of relationship may work out best for you, followed by a quiz designed to help you calculate your chances of a successful marriage.

I hope this book helps to lift the guilt from the shoulders of those who feel they have failed in their relationships and offers some hope for the future. What's more if you are single, what do you expect from a mate? Conversely do you expect too much? Fortunately there are those who are happily married, although it wouldn't do any harm to check out that it is happiness they are experiencing and not complacency or sheer laziness.

As the song says: "Love makes the world go round." And astrology, if used correctly, may make that orbit a smoother and happier one. And if it should raise a smile from a previously depressed reader, then this book will have justified its existence.

ARIES
(the Ram)

March 21 — April 20

Planet: Mars
Colour: Red
Partners: (In general) Leo, Sagittarius, Pisces
Countries: England, Denmark, Germany, Burgundy, Palestine, Syria, Japan
Cities: Birmingham, Oldham, Blackburn, Florence, Naples, Verona, Marseilles, Krakow, Brunswick
Famous Arietians: Doris Day, Gregory Peck, Charlie Chaplin, Hayley Mills, Thomas Jefferson, Vincent Van Gogh, Warren Beatty, Julie Christie, David Frost

---

GENERAL CHARACTERISTICS

If you were born between the above dates then your Sun is in the sign Aries, where it is at its most brilliant. The fire in you should be obvious to those close to you, who cannot have failed to notice your sense of adventure, aggression and ambition. In your career you may need to find another Arietian or someone with several planets in Aries before you can get the breaks you need. Your problem is that if you are unable to find a sympathetic ear or the chance to develop your ideas immediately, then other ideas you find equally challenging take their place. For this reason it is hard for you, once you run into difficulties, to persist in one course. Instead you scatter yourself over a wide front, taking only a surface interest in everything — hardly a recipe for success. Learn to fix your eyes on one ambition at a time, and stick to it like chewing-gum to a shoe. And what happens when you do finally emerge triumphant? Well, you are unlikely to be satisfied unless you have others following after you. You are the trail-blazing pioneer, the intrepid leader, but you prefer to leave it to someone else to build the settlement and maintain order. It is extremely rare for you to see through to the bitter end that which you start. Rather you are off exploring yet another tantalizing prospect. Because you like to be in a position of authority, you will leave home early in order to establish a family of your own, or else you may start your own business or go into a field where you can be the boss.

You are eternally optimistic and young at heart. Your enthusiasm is so contagious that you easily inspire other people. But — and it is a big but — you want everything your own way and should try not to be so imperious and domineering. Otherwise others will rebel, you can count on it! In private life Aries women particularly like to run the whole show, and are often too dictatorial and fiercely self-sufficient.

Frequently your independence is difficult to distinguish from insane rashness: you wilfully and impulsively fly headlong into a project or situation before you have investigated its dangers and possibilities sufficiently. This spur-of-the-moment action usually results in regret. It is fortunate, you may think, that you can conveniently forget your mistakes; but consider how much better it might be if you could learn from them.

With all that flaming energy it might be too much to expect you to control your passions. More often than not, you commit excesses and there is a tendency to take your body for granted and work it into the ground. You are generally careless about your health, placing too much strain on the weakest part of your body or ignoring the need to slow down when you are ill. In this way, you aggravate the ailment and then weak Arietians suffer from fevers, apoplexy or violent headaches.

In general, if others do not accept your rules you want your ball back and do not want to play the game. Life could be so much more pleasant if you learned to consider other people just a little bit more. After all, what can you lose? You are intelligent enough to realize that the only enemy you have is yourself.

ARIES AND MARRIAGE

Despite all the faults your mate may feel you possess, and the accusations of thoughtlessness and selfishness, at least no one can ever accuse you of being dishonest in a relationship, marriage or otherwise. Self-deceived — well, yes! naïve — possibly; but dishonest — no way! You enter this happy state in the same frame of mind as you start everything else: stirred by a thumping heart and a thought for new challenge. But what happens when the old ticker beats a little quieter, and what seemed like a trip into the unknown deteriorates into the chores of everyday life? You know as well as I do – you begin to lose interest, and either channel your energy into work or look around for a new romantic field to plough. What to eat for dinner is something you prefer not to think about; meals should miraculously appear at the appropriate hour. Shopping, paying the tradesmen — ah, you have bigger fish to fry. As for picking the kids up from school: "Can't we get a nanny, a maid? Anyone, but don't interrupt me!" Thoughts of how your minions should be paid rarely occur. Arguments over money, then, are only one of the problems which beset the Arietian in wedlock.

Sex, which once was a joy, can also become a bit of a headache. You will make love when *you* want to, and the more successful and demanding your career, the less often this is. It is hard for you to understand that making love need not always be instigated by mad passion, but that it can, after the exchange and discussion of mutual problems, be therapeutic and help to soothe away worries. An escape, if you like, but cheaper than booze and much more pleasant. There is nothing to beat it for calming nerves, giving reassurance, stimulating creativity and reawakening dulled emotions. Beats a prescription from the doctor any time!

You usually want to take too much out of a marriage instead of putting something in. "But I'm in favour of marriage," you cry. Yes, and that's why you try it again, and again and again. Your chances of success would greatly improve if in the first place you chose someone you liked as well as loved, with whom you could share your worries, a person who understood the things you want from life. In other words the communication lines need to be wide open. It's also a good idea at least to make an attempt at discovering your prospective mate's faults and ask yourself if you could accept them. There can only be three alternatives: yes, in time, or never. If the answer is a definite "yes", then advance with thumping heart. If "in time" or "never", hang around for a while before taking the final plunge; it will save you tears, bruised emotions and alimony or maintenance later.

ARIES HUSBAND

If you are looking for a playmate with the energy of a powerhouse then this is your man. Most women are impressed by his masculinity and daring. It is so easy to fall under his spell, although there are certain types of women who should make for the nearest exit when he charges into their lives.

Type I: The women's liberationist. He will respect her need to carve out her own career, no problems there. But even if she is Chairwoman of ICI she will still be expected to clean the house, bear his children and refrain from pestering him with domestic problems. When she dares to enquire exactly how and when she is to tackle all of this, he clams up, but it is probably during her lunch break! True, with both partners working they should be able to afford some help. But he thinks of himself as the leader, the boss, and in his opinion he must come first with his woman. Therefore she is supposed to actually enjoy washing his mildewy socks, rushing to the shops after work only to discover they have just closed. And, most important, she must present him with a sumptuous meal prepared by her own lily-white and overworked hands.

Type 2: The one-hundred-per-cent female woman should also put on running shoes when the Aries man approaches. He will be delighted when she rushes around in her frills and bows preparing a feast for him. He will be proud of the way she keeps the kids clean and tidy, but this feminine lady also tends to be pretty demanding emotionally. There she is, dressed to kill having finally got the kids into bed at seven o'clock, when the phone rings: "Won't be long, darling, I'm at a meeting." Brr Brr — eight o'clock: "Just got to explain to old Simpkins about the so-and-so project." Brr Brr — nine o'clock: "Hang on, darling, on my way home." Ten o'clock — nothing; eleven o'clock — silence. Twelve o'clock — she puts on a frilly nightie and takes a drink to bed. Finally he arrives. "Don't mind if I leave washing and shaving just this once, do you? I'm whacked, darling." She pours yet another drink. Two o'clock — from her side of the bed: "Sniff, sniff, you don't love me any more." Him ZZZZ. Sooner or later that drink becomes a little larger and is taken more frequently, and eventually she will not even notice whether he is there or not. Besides, that new repair man down the road has got the most beautiful eyes ...

Of course, there is the credit side to the Aries husband, for the right girl. With encouragement and enthusiasm he will work hard in his career, they will never starve even if it is up to her to make some kind of sense of the household bills. He will also be unquestionably loyal to the right lady, and a delight to watch romping on the floor with the kids, or with her for that matter — when he is home, that is. And if she is ever in trouble then he will willingly take up the gauntlet on her behalf, providing he feels her problems are real and important enough to warrant his valuable attention.

You will love him, hate him, but one thing is for sure: you can't ignore him.

ARIES WIFE

Have you again been overlooked for promotion? Are you lacking in a professional direction in life? Then here is the answer. The Aries woman can organize anyone or anything; all she needs is the chance. She is an expert at delivering the well-aimed kick when her man is letting life get on top of him. And she has unquestionable faith in his abilities or you can be sure she would not have married him in the first place. She will gouge, bite and punch him up the ladder of success even sometimes when he does not want to get up there. And if he is not the ambitious type, then why the hell did he marry an Aries woman? She can take the most worthless tramp and turn him into a man his mother would be proud of. These are the talents given to her and she is not about to waste them. Her man can also be sure that life will not get dull, even if she decides of her own volition to give up her own career; but please don't expect her to play the little woman. She will join this committee or that club and will be busy organizing the neighbourhood or her friends, or both. She must have scope for her abundant energy. She can handle the house, the kids, her man and her friends blindfolded, so she has plenty of time for outside activity.

Now this is all very fine and commendable if these services and talents are required, but maybe they are not. It is conceivable that she may have married a perfectly efficient and capable man, who is able to steer his career without any back-seat driving from her, thank you very much! If this does happen, our heroine is in trouble. She retaliates and either returns to work in an effort to compete with her husband, or her splendid energy is channelled into endless other attempts to dominate the relationship. Heaven help the man with an Aries wife whose sole motivation to work is to get even with him. If she becomes successful, then he will be playing a very poor second to her professional problems. She will show him that HER job is far more worthwhile, important etc., than his. Marriage in such circumstances can hardly be expected to thrive and, sooner or later, she will run across an attractive man with a promising new talent or executive ability, one who could no doubt benefit from her experience and guidance. Once this happens, sometime in the near future one Aries lady will be making a rapid escape. It may be, of course, her husband who suddenly runs into a dishy neighbour while sorting out some domestic problem that she was too busy to attend to. But either way leads to the divorce courts.

Ideally, then, the Aries female needs not exactly a weak man but certainly one who is not adverse to being organized. So when those palpitations begin she should ask herself not "Can I help or manage this man?" but "Will he mind my doing so?"

ARIES AND DIVORCE

Divorce is hardly a stranger to this sign. A broken marriage may seem to have caused plenty of pain, but at least Arietians are gifted or plagued — depending on your point of view — with a sufficiently short memory as to make unpleasantness easy to forget. Aries divorces are rarely prolonged and painful. If there is one thing you are good at, it is bringing to an end something for which you have no further use. Your departure is swift; you don't hang around waiting for recriminations or the task of sorting out mutual possessions. If there is anything you want to hang on to, you let your solicitor obtain it for you. Even deserted and humiliated Arietians recover once their pride is soothed. Yes, you are quick to pick yourself up, dust yourself off and charge in once more, your faith in marriage shaken not a bit.

Where other more determined signs would prefer to sort out their problems, those born under Aries would prefer to start again rather than put effort into making an ailing relationship work. Having decided a person belongs in your past, then you don't expect him or her to play an important part in your future. Male Arietians are particularly good at cutting off a wife and family. This does not make them heartless; they just frequently decide that this is preferable to dividing up the kids like merchandise. Your Arietian personality, together with the fact that you don't regard divorce as insufferable, makes it easy to understand why you may experience it several times.

ARIES EX-HUSBAND

As an ex-husband you usually get full marks. You are unlikely to sidestep your financial responsibilities; not that you would volunteer to give up hard-earned cash, but you will pay up as long as demands are reasonable and, of course, while you are working. But if you should fall on hard times and that ex-wife of yours continues to apply pressure, then your fighting instinct will surface and you will either go to court and attempt to get your liabilities reduced or simply disappear from view, reappearing later when life has improved like a belated Santa Claus laden with peace offerings and toys. And when your welcome is anything but warm, you will be confused and hurt. Regrettably, as an ex-husband you have one drawback. If you have not found yourself a new love, then you may be tempted to see if there is anything you can do to stoke up old fires. However, one rejection is usually enough to send you running home with your tail between your legs.

When your former spouse decides to remarry, out of curiosity you will contrive a way to get a glimpse of your successor just once, simply to convince yourself that he does not come up to your own impeccable standard. But you are not the type who believes in so-called civilized behaviour. You know the kind of thing: "Darling, I want you to meet my ex-wife. She has improved so much since I became her friend instead of her husband." Or: "This is my present wife — she is a definite step forward, don't you think?" That fierce pride of yours is no doubt beginning to rebel even at the thought of it. No, as far as you are concerned, once both of you are reclaimed, then, apart from the financial considerations, you would rather make a graceful retreat. Yet there is no doubt about it, as an ex-husband you are difficult to beat. You are around if needed and happy to disappear when not. Continuing bitchiness or recriminations are not for you.

ARIES EX-WIFE

The role of ex-wife does not come easily to you, although given time you may achieve perfection. Your ex-hubby may have departed because of your domineering behaviour, but just because you are now divorced, there is no reason for you to lose interest in his achievement. Besides, you never know, there may be something you can do to help him — Right? WRONG! No matter how long it may take to sink in, you must accept the fact that he is quite capable of finding his own way. Even if he is not, it certainly is not up to you to interfere unless asked. You are the type who if invited to attend a little party he is throwing will, upon arrival, pounce on his present love and expound on his inability to add up two and two, only to be informed that he has just obtained a degree in higher mathematics — that is, if you are asked at all. Once you find a new love of your own to worry about, then you may leave the poor man in peace. However, before you take over your latest love, shouldn't you discover whether he wants you to? If he does, O.K. then away you go. But take it easy, or the term ex-wife may be one you will be acquiring several times.

Despite all this, it can be said in your favour that being fiercely independent you will work and slave until you can support the kids and the house without any help from that rat. And one day when your ex-old man is counting his blessings, on reflection he may even count you in there with the rest of them. Who knows, you may eventually become popular with your successor, providing you keep your distance. As an ex-wife then there are certainly worse. But it is not a title you enjoy or intend to keep for long. You need someone in your life, and you know it!

ARIES AND COHABITATION

Arietians are generally pro marriage, although there may be periods when you perhaps feel that once or twice bitten, three of four times shy. While this mood prevails you could well decide to set up home with your lover in order to observe him or her in the throes of everyday life. A good idea, as long as you remember that it works both ways: you will also be on trial. If after eighteen months you can still feel that adrenalin surging through you, despite the fact that she wears so much cold cream at night that she slips out of your arms, or that his foot-rot is so overpowering that his socks run screaming to the laundry basket, then it would appear that you are on to a good thing. Conversely, stifle disillusionment if your Romeo or Juliet fails to come up to scratch. Instead be grateful that you refrained from tying a legal knot, and when bruised emotions have finally healed, try again. You are not that impossible to please. It is simply that you possess a passionate but indiscriminate heart. If anything surpasses the speed at which you become emotionally involved, it is the records you break as you struggle to become disentangled. A trial relationship is a realistic proposition for those born under this sign, although not surprisingly complications can arise when children are involved; you can hardly subject them to a steady stream of prospective mummies or daddies and expect them to grow into well adjusted adults. They can also make it almost impossible for you to get acquainted with your lover. The constant patter of tiny feet or the thump of wellington boots does not exactly make for privacy. You may even develop a totally distorted idea of your lover's personality. With reservations, I believe that providing you are childless, then by all means go ahead and get it together. If you are a parent, you will need to be as sure of your new love as it is humanly possible to be. Introduce your man or lady to the kids, and if you survive the experience without broken bones, then gradually increase the visits. If you are all still neurosis-free after a couple of months, then give it a whirl. But a word of warning: if Mr or Miss Wonderful begins to display panic symptoms and utter doubts regarding his or her ability to take on a ready-made family, then face up to it, my Aries friend, you have boobed yet again. However, do remember that there is another side to this particular coin: if you cannot accept your lover's kids, then no amount of picnics or trips to the cinema with them will help. The kindest thing that you can do is evaporate before you hurt not just your lover and yourself but also one, two or three innocent parties who do not deserve it.

ARIES AND THE COMMUNE

Unless the other members of the commune are prepared to stand down and offer the Arietian leadership, then this is a preposterous idea. Generally speaking, this is not a lifestyle for the ram. Those who adopt this way of life must share, something which does not come easily to this character. Such an existence is strictly out unless the community concerned is ready for dictatorship, in which case life will be run with the usual Arietian efficiency. Everyone will be allotted daily instructions to be carried out to the letter. But don't expect to catch the Arietian with dirty hands; he is the organizer and the thought this requires leaves little time for actual hard labour. Even if it were possible for the ram to serve in this capacity, the commune life is hardly the ideal existence for him. Mainly because when he issues orders his manner leaves a lot to be desired and he generally causes hostility with his bumptious behaviour. It can only be a matter of time before a coup d'état takes place and our friend is deposed, the tranquil atmosphere now completely destroyed. Communal life and Aries are simply not compatible.

ARIES LOVER — MALE

The Arietian lover is a tantalizing proposition. Some say he is playful, immature and passionate; others believe him to be over-sexed and gushing. In all cases, you clearly need to be reminded that if you are setting up house with eventual view to marriage then you may not be able to play Romeo constantly. It is imperative for you both that you can be yourselves for better and worse. Otherwise how on earth can either of you ascertain whether your relationship is strong enough to survive as a base for marriage? This does not provide you with an excuse to turn into a slob, far from it: romance needs to be kept intermittently very much alive.

Finances should also be tackled as though you were already hitched or you may never discover whether you can agree on the distribution of mutual monies. There are those who believe that one must work harder at a relationship which is not sanctified by a piece of paper. This, of course, is a generalization. In fact some people rebel against being told one is supposed to behave or react in any way. You as an Aries may well appreciate this. After all, it should be relatively easy for you to cohabit with someone you love, effort only occasionally being required. Should a relationship be constant hard work, then something is seriously wrong.

Initially your lover will believe that you are the wittiest, cleverest and most romantic man she has ever met. If this belief persists for a year, then perhaps you should tie the knot quickly before she changes her mind. If you effortlessly continue to display the more pleasant side of your nature, you will have something of real value. But whatever else you do, never rush into marriage after a few idyllic weeks. Consistency isn't exactly one of your strong points. Your latest playmate may seem perfect now, but in six months you could well begin to think of her as Godzilla.

ARIES LOVER — FEMALE

When you enter domestic bliss with an Aries woman, the first thing to impress you will be her efficiency. If after six months it has not begun to irritate you, then you may be well-matched. Sexually speaking, she will certainly keep you on your toes so long as she retains her respect for you. But no one should expect an Aries female to revolve her whole world around her man; this must be accepted if your love is to lead anywhere apart from to loneliness. The right amount of freedom will inspire her into giving, something that doesn't come naturally. In the correct conditions she will happily accept her share of responsibility, but give her enough rein and before you know what has happened she will take over completely. She is not the insanely jealous type if she has no reason to doubt you; if you say you are working late, she will believe you. Her faith is touching.

If you decide to postpone marriage for a few years, only to be confronted one evening by her maternal instinct, there is no need to panic. A legal piece of paper won't prevent her from having your child, if this is what you both want. She is not restricted by convention and feels perfectly capable of coping on her own should it ever become necessary. In fact she may be so self-sufficient that you find yourself wondering why you are there at all; it is a deeply ingrained part of her personality and one you must adapt to, otherwise find the nearest exit.

She ain't going to change. The Aries woman needs a special kind of man and it could take quite a while before she makes contact with him.

Lastly, if she is a doting mother, then you are about to be thrown in at the deep end. You will be expected to take on your share of domestic chores, and she has little patience. She will demonstrate ONCE how to change the baby's rear end, then you are on your own. Clearly this is not a woman for the faint-hearted. It is possible I may have made the Aries woman sound a rather daunting prospect; if this is how it strikes you, then you are clearly not for her, so step aside and allow someone else to try his luck.

ARIES CHILD AND DIVORCE

The disappearance of one parent from the matrimonial home is more easily accepted by the young Aries child than, say, the Cancerian or the Scorpion. Neither is there any need to insult his or her intelligence by telling fairy stories. The simple truth without gory details is readily understood by this little character. Providing the missing parent can make regular and punctual visits, the Aries child will not sink into deep neurosis or insecurity and in fact in no time at all will have worked out how to extract the maximum from both worlds. The teenage Arietian, however, like all teenagers labours through several insecure years and a divorce at this point could completely floor them. This teenager may scorn advice but certainly expects to receive it. After all, without those monotonous parental pearls of wisdom, what is there to rebel against? And the young Arietian learns, how to fight early in life; it is as natural as breathing. An obedient teenage Arietian is one with problems. It just isn't natural for this sign. Regardless of age, there will always be a determined loyalty to the missing parent, which needs to be recognized and accepted. The sure way to lose this child is to fill his/her ears with tales about the "rat" or "bitch" who left you, for in no time at all communication will become blocked. If Mum or Dad really was so bad the child will find out when mature enough to cope; even then, don't be surprised if he or she remains doggedly loyal. You may be bringing up this character alone in the face of great opposition, working your fingers to the bone, but don't expect applause for your efforts. Your offspring will still infuriate you by insisting on hero-worshipping that worthless ex of yours, but grit your teeth and struggle on. It is a natural Arietian reaction, nothing to visit the psychiatrist about. That kicking, screaming bundle is perfectly normal, so relax.

ARIES CHILD AND REMARRIAGE

Remarriage should not present any lasting problems, provided the new parent never tries to exorcise the adored predecessor from the Arietian child's heart, or demand instant recognition of the changed situation. You will need to discover what interests the youngster and endeavour to become an expert in that particular field. Little gems of information can then be dropped into casual conversation over the ensuing months. Initially you may not think this has made any impression, but watch carefully and you will see definite curiosity. The child will decide when the time is ripe to approach you for advice or help, and this will occur only when the conclusion is that the new parent is not such a drip after all ... When the first advance is finally made, the talk should be illuminating but brief, and it will not be long before the young Arietian returns with more questions. Once a mutual interest is out in the open, various outings with the child can be arranged. If the new parent has swotted up on stamps, for example, then a trip to view some rare specimens will be a great step forward in the relationship.

Knowing what to do about discipline is hard, particularly if the new parent is the father. Obviously he can't walk in and start throwing his weight around. Rather he needs to back up the real parent all the way down the line, and after a while it is permissible for him to add a few of his own reproaches. In my opinion, it is important for a new father to take over the discipline just as soon as the relationship allows. A weak father figure makes for confused children, a resentful wife and World War III at home. The Aries child needs to respect both parents; it could well take a "hot bottom" to achieve this. A sense of justice is essential with all kids, and in this case it is of paramount importance, as is a kiss and a cuddle at bedtime, providing it is done naturally. It is only a matter of time before this child realizes that in many ways having three or even four parents can be great fun.

CONCLUSION
After this examination of the pros and cons of various relationships, the poor Arietian may be feeling that he simply does not fit in anywhere. It is necessary to set his mind at rest and suggest the most successful road for him to follow.

The commune? The odds must be two in a million against success in this way of life. Cohabitation then? Fine for a while, but too insecure for a permanent arrangement. The Darby-and-Joan syndrome? Out of character. Bachelorhood? Again, maybe for a while, but the Aries needs someone to dominate.

It does not leave us with much, does it? In fact, as a member of this sign, you have probably already found the answer. The only way you can proceed in life is, of course, through marriage. But it needs to be undertaken with an honest Arietian approach; in other words, you must accept that it will possibly not last. However, by marrying more cautiously, and perhaps living beforehand with prospective husband or wife, you may cut down your failure rate from four to say two. A small percentage of Arietians may even find a marriage that lasts for ever, but don't rely on it. If the conventional members of the human race display shock when you state that you have been divorced a couple of times, perhaps they should consider that in many cases it may be the only answer. For example, you as an Arietian may rush into matrimony only to discover that your mate possesses a homosexual leaning which develops strongly over the years. What are you supposed to do? And what about the starry-eyed girl who later discovers that her man simply cannot cope with the pressures of life and turns into a wife beater? Must she be expected to stick around? She may, if there is a masochistic side to her character — indeed some women judge the depth of hubby's love by the number of black eyes they receive in one week. But a normal Arietian- is not about to stick around in such circumstances.

However, just as there are many good reasons for a divorce so are there many bad. "He put his cold feet on my back, Your Honour," and similar get-outs are frequently used by Arietians. Maybe the poor man was trying to attract attention. As I said, there are situations where divorces are necessary and where they are unnecessary. Arietians should try to ensure that they belong to the latter group, if only to cut down the number of divorces and the amount of alimony. After all, a man with four ex-wives and several kids to support is not exactly increasing his chances of happiness and is certainly making life tough for number five. One ex-wife, two at the outside, should be enough for anyone — although I doubt that the Arietian is even paying attention at this point. He needs to be reminded that a successful married life does not mean forty years of misery with the same person. If, as a member of this sign, you managed to get through, say, two divorces and are now happy with several well-adjusted children, then I reckon you have done pretty well. No one is perfect, and that includes you!

ARIES MARRIAGE CHANCES QUIZ

Answer honestly the questions below and score 3 for yes, 2 for sometimes or unsure and 1 for no.

1. Do you fall in love easily?
2. In retrospect are you often amazed at the passion you felt for a past love?
3. Could you allow your lover to end your relationship without recriminations?
4. Is it difficult for you to restrain yourself once in love?
5. Do you expect your mate's life to revolve around you?
6. Do you believe that divorce is a perfectly acceptable way to solve differences?
7. Do you get impatient with day-to-day problems?
8. Are you impulsive?
9. Are you forceful with your mate?
10. Do you value your freedom?

11. Do you believe in marriage?
12. Are you a romantic?
13. Do you believe in living for today?
14. Is sex an important part of marriage to you?
15. Does the domesticity of marriage worry you?
16. While emotionally involved, are you faithful?
17. Do you tend to shelve problems until you are in the right frame of mind?
18. Do you have difficulty remembering sentimental dates?
19. Do you take the initiative in relationships?
20. Did your love life begin before the age of sixteen?

ANSWERS

1 — 30: Although you may have some Arietian tendencies, your score suggests that several planets on your personal birth chart occupy Scorpio, Cancer or Pisces. Because of this, you take marriage more seriously than the average Arietian. Also you are far more cautious about taking the step in the first place, and therefore your chances of finding a successful marriage are increased. You would take quite a time to recover from divorce and might avoid a further legal attachment altogether, preferring cohabitation.

31 — 50: This is the score of an Arietian in possession of the better characteristics of the sign. Your strong personality indicates that you know exactly what you want in life and love and can for the most part obtain it without hurting other people. However, you are always true to yourself and this may foul up at least one marriage. If married before the age of twenty-five, then two marriages are predicted for you.

51 — 60: You are a true Arietian for good and bad. Your strong independence organizing and the "me first" characteristics don't exactly contribute to a happy marital life. You are in and out of relationships with frightening speed. All this combined with the ability to attract the opposite sex like flies is guaranteed to lead you into the divorce court several times. Do try to be more cautious and discriminating.

TAURUS
(the Bull)
April 21 — May 21

Planet: Venus
Colour: Blue or pink
Partners: (In general) Virgo and Capricorn
Countries: Ireland, Persia, Poland, Georgia, Cyprus
Cities: Dublin, Palma, Rhodes, St Louis
Famous Taureans: Shakespeare, Margot Fonteyn, Henry Fonda, Barbra Streisand, Audrey Hepburn, Robert Browning, Perry Como, Bing Crosby, Tchaikovsky, Fred Astaire

---

GENERAL CHARACTERISTICS

If your birthday falls between the above dates, you have your Sun in Taurus. You are not as mentally active as your Arietian friends but you certainly have a large dose of good common sense. Neither the idealist nor dreamer, you are cautious, constructive and stable. You never expect a windfall, but rather the just rewards of steady application to your appointed work. Your motto is "one foot after another" until the goal is reached, and it is in the end responsible for your solid success.

You are industrious, patient and practical. A conservative first and foremost, you like to identify with the traditional, the tried and true. Once you have made up your mind, you stick stubbornly to a course of action. You are not afraid of hard work; in fact, you are dedicated to it. Obstacles only make you more persistent. For this reason, you are an excellent boss or a conscientious devoted employee.

You have untold amounts of reserve energy and are capable of waiting a long time for your plans to mature. Sometimes you are overly tenacious and can stick to a losing cause long after others know it to be hopeless. You become obstinate, even violently enraged, when other people try to drive you into doing something, though you are perfectly amenable if they appeal to you in the right way. You are placid, domesticated and very affectionate. Taurean love affairs may begin passionately but they develop into warm, friendly relationships that are ideal for a happily settled marriage. You are usually a faithful and contented spouse.

You are sound and reliable in financial dealings and would make an excellent banker, manager or trustee. You appreciate both money and the possessions it buys. You have an innate sense of beauty but prefer art objects that are also useful. You may also like jewellery, to wear yourself or to give to your mate. Necklaces are likely to be a first choice.

You have great physical endurance, but once you succumb to a disease you may be slow to recuperate. If Taurus works against you on your individual chart, you may be clumsy. Taurus rules the throat, neck, shoulders and base of the brain, and you could have trouble in any one of these areas. In general you accept life more calmly and take better care of yourself than those of other signs. The negative type of Taurean may be lazy, luxury-loving and self-indulgent, and all types have to resist a tendency to overeat and overimbibe. You find it hard to deny yourself pleasures connected with the throat.

It is probable that you learn more from experience than from what you read or were taught at school. While being theoretically very constructive, you place a high value on having the necessary practical knowledge before attempting a project. Slowly, steadily, surely, you build a solid structure, flattening all opposition as inevitably as a steam-roller and not being distracted from your purpose by side issues. Some Taureans may not communicate easily in speech or writing, although they do have strong feelings to express. For this reason, you may appear stolid or phlegmatic to others. However, those of you with planets in Aries or Gemini are usually able to overcome this difficulty.

The artistic and musical side of this sign means many Taureans have memorable voices or a knowledge of art objects and antiques. You are particularly attached to your personal possessions and may be very proud of them for their aesthetic as well as their realizable value. Your religious beliefs are down-to-earth and practical; you are also devout, warm-hearted and sincere. Nevertheless you must be careful not to be so impressed with the forms of religion that you overlook their actual meaning. Keats's creed "Beauty is truth, truth beauty" may well be your own.

TAURUS AND MARRIAGE
Physical attraction is very important to you. Platonic love hardly

exists. You are natural and direct in any love relationship and your instincts are so pure that you have no sense of shame. Although you were probably a late developer physically, you would always have attracted plenty of admirers. However, you don't fall in love until the right person arrives; you know at once when this happens, and you usually love for life. In this respect the Bull is quite conventional. Once you have found your mate, you are tremendously faithful, affectionate and demonstrative. You like gifts, love letters, flowers — all the accoutrements of love.

It is a rare Bull who charges into marriage in the teens; your late development plus your strong sense of caution usually help you avoid such a mistake. Neither is your marriage the result of a dreamy courtship. True, you may recognize the right person immediately, but practical considerations tend to delay the actual marriage. These characteristics contribute to the fact that of all the signs Taurus subjects have a lower divorce rate. Taureans play for keeps and are unimpressed by the so-called swinging lifestyles of bachelor friends. To you a good time probably means an evening spent alone with your man or woman, with a good meal and lots and lots of love.

However, there is one aspect to your personality that could set your relationship floundering on to the rocks. There is a real danger that you will let your sense of well-being deteriorate into a taking of your loved one for granted, then before you know where you are your spouse is marching out of the door. You need to fight an inclination to become too domesticated. If you prefer staying at home, then at least throw regular little get-togethers with friends. And when there are kids you should make a point of allowing them twice a year to stay with doting nanny while you both escape to some little hotel in a romantic setting. It will do wonders for your flagging relationship. If this is out of the question for practical reasons, then stay at home and plan a few surprises for your lover: some culinary treats, romantic and sexual delights. Don't imagine that because you have caught a mate for life they wholly belong to you physically and emotionally.

The pressures of work plus financial headaches will periodically weigh you down, and not unexpectedly the first side to your relationship to suffer will be the sexual. Remember, just as you can easily adapt to and expect sex three times a day so you can drift into abstinence — excluding birthdays, of course. In other words, Taureans are lazy lovers. Why not discuss with your mate money problems or the professional dramas you are experiencing? Then ease your stress in the arms of your opposite number. This will give you added impetus and resilience when coping with the pressures of the outside world.

Despite your faults, if you as a Taurean cannot make a success of marriage then there is little hope for the rest of us. The very institution was probably founded by a member of your sign.

TAURUS HUSBAND

If you are looking for a bread-winner who will never let you down, a man who has not even noticed the sex-bomb living down the road, and a man who is capable of complete devotion to the right female, then please form an orderly queue, here he is — the perfect husband ...

But wait. Is that a liberated woman I spot down there on the right? Then I am sorry, there is no point in your actually waiting around to have your heart trampled on. Not unless you are the bionic woman, and you would need to be. This character will fight you tooth and nail if you wish to carry on a career after the wedding bells have been rung; even if he should eventually relent — which is highly unlikely — it will only be on the condition that your work does not interfere with your marriage or raising the kids. "I have won," you may think; but reconsider. You will never be able to wail over your work problems, let alone expect sympathy. He will agree to getting you someone to help with the children or around the house. But the moment the daily woman is caught with her hands in your liquor or little John goes down with a temperature, guess who will be blamed? Right first time. It would have never happened if you had been there. He will make you feel like a neglectful wife and a cruel, heartless mother. Chances are you will eventually leave work; the aggravation just won't be worth it. No, my liberated friend, the Taurean man is not for you. Try Mr Gemini or possibly Mr Sagittarius.

Who is next? Ah, yes, the feminine lady. Are you the type who likes to abide by her man's wishes? You are? Good. And you adore whipping up a perfect soufflé at a moment's notice? Splendid. Do you get a kick out of totally belonging to your man? Affirmative, great. Then step forward, you are just the girl this character has been looking for.

If you are still with me, Taurean man, you may consider that I am being unjust. Not a bit of it. You do have your faults, you know, just like the rest of us, and it does no harm to be honest about them. Oh, it does? Pardon me. I will leave this section then, before you go into one of your famous stampedes.

TAURUS WIFE

Are you the type of man who likes to arrive home and be greeted by a low neckline and a high-rise lemon meringue pie? Do you need someone to clasp you to her ample bosom, kiss away your professional frustrations and soothe your bruised ego before returning to the big wide world refreshed? If you are, then you have got the right birth sign: the Taurean lady is excellent marriage material and she knows it, therefore, she is not about to get lumbered with just anyone. She puts a high price on her freedom and so she should. Apart from being an excellent cook, mother and bed companion, she will never squander your hard-earned cash. In fact, if you are pretty hopeless at juggling the finances, then leave it to her. She can be relied upon not to spend the electricity money on a new dress. Likewise, she will be horrified if you spend money on a night out with the boys. Not that she is likely to allow you out on your own, you understand; this is a possessive lady and she needs the physical presence of her man even if she sometimes behaves as if you did not exist. That's a strange thing about this sign: Taureans are so practical and sensible, but when a marriage begins to rock, does she accept the fact and do something about it? No. As far as she is concerned, nothing is wrong. I suppose if hubby came home at three o'clock every morning, reeking of perfume and with lipstick plastered all over him, she might get a slight suspicion, but she is more likely to be conveniently asleep. This way she does not have to admit that their relationship might be falling apart. I guess the satin panties found in the car could be the last straw. In this instance, what does she do? She lets rip with a few piercing screams, several threats, but once this is off her chest, she will proceed to tell herself that everything is fine. Well, isn't it? This lady clings to relationships long after they have died. It is probably a reluctance to admit to having made a mistake. Assurances that all is well will echo even while she ascends the steps of the divorce court, but that is the Taurean — strong, determined, stubborn and bloody-minded.

TAURUS AND DIVORCE

Divorce is an unhappy occurrence for the Taurean. Fortunately many born under this sign escape the experience altogether, while others may face it just once (neither do they want to hear about your friend who is currently on number six). Taureans' divorces are often prolonged and painful affairs mainly because it is so difficult for them to let go. We have all read about the character who refuses to budge from his ex-wife's doorstep until forcibly removed by the law. I bet that unhappy man is a Taurean! Most Taureans' marriages are pretty lengthy before terminated, and this makes it even harder. Many Bulls never completely recover, and some can only go through the whole thing once; they therefore shy away from emotional entanglement altogether. The best help or comfort I can offer to Taurean divorcees is this: because of your ability to endure and give yourself, if you should be lucky enough to fall in love again, then quite suddenly you will be amazed that you clung on to that ex-spouse so long. Life goes on, you will say, and this time you will mean it. But don't despair if for a while it seems impossible for you to imagine life without that erring spouse. With you, time is definitely the healer. If you do rush into an early remarriage, then your motives will be questionable. It might be nice for the kids to have a new mother or father, and yes, you could do with some help with the bills. But you are the type who needs a lot more from a relationship, so allow yourself a recovery period. You don't want to go through the whole sticky mess again, do you?

TAURUS EX-HUSBAND

As an ex-husband, you are not exactly the bargain of the month. You may be top as a marriage prospect, but your value is greatly reduced once the decree absolute has been granted. It is true that you invariably pay out the alimony; you may even slip in some extra. But why do you have to pamper and bribe the kids in order to discover what she is up to, and couldn't you telephone before arriving uninvited at the old matrimonial home? Of course, you will argue, your actions are guided by the best of motives; someone has to protect her from the gigolo she is now running around with, and, besides, it is not pleasant to discover that her reputation has been torn to shreds by the neighbours. But why not give her some credit? After all, she married you, didn't she? Therefore, she can't be a complete fool. Anyway, perhaps the gigolo is fun, and marriage to you may not have been. "But she looked so ill," you protest. Well, maybe that is due to the late nights. Besides there is always the mother-in-law to watch over her little baby. Think about yourself, will you? You must be sensible. Let's face it, she may rush out and get married again tomorrow. She doesn't need your permission, you know. It is no good kidding yourself she is still in love with you and always will be. Of course, you will always feel something but if you don't let her alone, it could be disgust and resentment. Once you have found yourself someone else, even if it is only an infatuation, you will feel better, and I doubt that you would appreciate the same interference from her.

In the meantime, take a look in the mirror. Is that the beginning of a pouch? And how old is that suit — five, six or seven years? You can't regain your youth, but a change of image would not be a bad idea. You are a bachelor again, and there is a whole wide world full of gorgeous women. Smarten yourself up and get out there. Maybe your hairdresser could think of a more flattering style, a touch more youthful perhaps. A health club would also go a long way to tone up those muscles. Ask yourself whether you looked like this when your ex fell for you. I doubt it. Taureans do tend to let themselves go. Shape up there; life can be fun again, it only requires a little effort. You will soon adapt to your new status and, in six months, wonder why you were so full of trepidation.

TAURUS EX-WIFE

The Taurean ex-wife is a similar animal to her male counterpart. This is not a status which brings out her finer qualities. Because she was such a devoted and loyal wife, she tends to think that she will make the "rat" pay for the wasted years, especially if he deserted her. He is not going to escape his responsibilities, oh, no! She gets out her Sherlock Holmes hat at intervals in an effort to establish how well he is doing. Every rise to fame or fortune is going to be a sixty-forty deal in her favour if she can get it. She is after every penny, cent or franc she can get, and if he remarries before her, then the pressure will be increased. How dare he throw her over for that little tramp? The only thing her ex can do is make attempts at finding her a man, for once she is remated, he will cease to bear the full force of her attention.

Like her brother Taurean, this lady is in danger of letting her appearance go. She also consumes vast amounts of food in order to compensate for emotional insecurity so the advice given to the male is applicable here. Don't slop around feeding your face while you plan all kinds of retributions. Take a good, hard, honest look at yourself. What would you look like in a bikini? On second thoughts don't answer that question. And what about that hair — how long is it since you have changed the style or the colour? You can't remember? Now turn sideways ... You may have worn a size 10 when that ex of yours swept you off your feet, but could you get into the same dress now? No, I thought not. What's the damage then? Size 12, 14, 16 if not an 18! No, it is no good blaming the "swine". It is just as much your fault as his. So come on, action is called for. Imagine his face if you could take the kids over to him wearing hot pants and a low neckline. No, of course you don't want him back — or do you? At least, let him see that he left a woman behind and not a pudding. Of course, your greatest incentive is a new love, and that will come in time. But if you sit around much longer, you will be a realistic candidate for fat lady in a circus. Are you going to let that ex of yours do that to you? Of course not. If you think of all the people in the world, and half of them are men, it stands to reason that there must be at least one with your label around his neck. A certain financial independence could also be a good thing, for while you are so dependent on him you may be put off ever getting hitched again. A change of attitude is called for, my girl. Right? Right.

TAURUS AND COHABITATION

This will not be the ideal arrangement for a Taurean mainly because in your case the relationship is likely to be based on all the wrong reasons. Where other signs set up home in order to learn more about each other, so that marriage may be considered or simply because they can't live apart any longer, you as a Taurus may enter this state for practical and financial considerations, especially if you have been married before. After all, the old alimony stops when she ties the knot again, doesn't it? And let's face it, it can't be bad having two men help you out with the cost of living. Even the male Taurean can easily accept the shadowy figure of an ex-husband if he has his hands in his pocket. The trouble is where does it end? One or other of you will want to put things on a more secure footing eventually. But sheer greed could prevent this from occurring. Of course, if you are the poor unfortunate who is paying out, then life is not much fun. Two electricity bills. Two gas bills. Rent. Phone. HELP! It is enough to make the Taurean male flee into a monastery. If you can't afford to run two homes, then you are sunk. You will either have to wait until the ex remarries, or choose an independent and rich girl, although it is doubtful that your ego will allow this.

Naturally if you and your lover are single and always have been, then these hang ups simply do not arise, and the problems are vastly different. If you have agreed to set up house together in order to see whether or not you would make feasible candidates for Darby and Joan, then life is uncomplicated. You will either make it or you won't, it is simple. If marriage is out of the question, then although the Taurean may he happy and content for a while, at some point insecurity will rear its head. "Why shouldn't we get married? You love me, don't you? And I want a family." "But we don't need a ring to have a family." "Oh, no, I couldn't possibly. Children should only arrive within the security of marriage. It might be a love child to you, but it would be a bastard to me. Where are you going, darling?" ... Crash! Slam! No I'm afraid this kind of relationship just won't work over a long period. You will need to think again.

TAURUS AND THE COMMUNE

For a limited period you could exist quite happily with this adopted lifestyle. As a Taurean, you tend to think of yourself as Mother or Father Earth so, with the large family to worry about, you could be quite happy. But while you may be only too willing to share your possessions and chores, you keep a jealous eye on your loved one. You would become suspicious if another male or female offered to repair your lady's sewing machine or if an attractive female showed a willingness to sew on your mate's shirt buttons. That rare but violent temper of yours would at some point flare up and wreak havoc on everyone and everything around you. It would be the quickest disintegration of the group you have ever witnessed. Mind you, this alternative way of life isn't totally out of the question. If you are in a rock-solid relationship and feel one hundred per cent secure, then you may just be able to make a go of it.

TAURUS LOVER — MALE

A secure Bull is a pleasure to behold. There he stands contentedly chewing the daisies and contemplating nature. This is the Taurean lover when his mate can satisfy his emotional and physical demands — demands that become excessive when he finds himself living in cohabitation. For a while, he may be able to cope with those little doubts and misgivings, but if the relationship should turn into a lengthy affair, then he can't understand why he should not be married. Statements like "I am not ready for that big step yet" or "I need time to get somewhere in the world before settling down" meet with an impatient snort. A few more choice remarks like this, and the Bull will stop chewing daisies and begin to paw the ground. It is probable that she will not recognize the danger symptoms 'til he is in full charge, and an angry Bull is not a happy sight. He is red-faced, the veins throb and stand out on his neck, steam pours out of his mouth and ears. Fortunately, this is a rare occurrence. She may live with him for two years believing him to be a placid old thing until that fatal day when he stampedes.

In short relationships, however, he is a joy — romantic, practical, a tower of strength and probably a better cook than she is. But the Bull is not the tidiest of creatures, so be warned. His every thought is for her comfort and well-being. It is easy to get used to having him around. The blood may have ceased to rush through her veins at the slightest mention of his name, but he is comfortable and she should be warned against marrying him simply because she can't imagine life without him. He may be big, powerful and strong, but he will hurt easily if she suddenly leaves him in order to follow a more exciting proposition.

TAURUS LOVER — FEMALE

As a lover, the Taurean lady makes a good mountaineer. But she tries, my God, how she tries! In the beginning, she rushes home from work, slips into something seductive and produces a meal a Cordon Bleu cook would be proud of, which, come to think of it, she probably is. They dine in candlelight and end the evening making beautiful love. This is not a treat, it is a regular occurrence. Then he suggests at some point that they should see a little more of the outside world. Why? Isn't she enough for him? She will laugh, but tears well up in those incredible eyes. He feels like a heel. Well, then, why don't they have some friends round? She is temporarily consoled and agrees. When the fatal evening arrives, she is such an excellent hostess that he puffs up with pride. That is until the guests have departed. Then it starts. How long has he been friends with Tom, Dick or Fred? And what about his date? Did he introduce them? Well, then how long has he known Sharon, Mary or Flossie? And is it necessary for him to be so affectionate with her? Not that she minds you understand, but Tom, Dick or Fred may get the wrong idea. Her husband vows never to invite friends home again. Next time they will go out. Mistake. Did he know that girl who was so interested in him at the restaurant? And why *that* restaurant? Does it have happy memories? Who did he take there? etc. ... No, don't misunderstand me, the Taurus lady is not normally so impossible. It is simply that after six months of cohabitation without even the slightest mention of marriage, it is beginning to worry her. The only way to go is either avoid living with this type at all or to limit yourself to six glorious months, although I would not like to be around when you decide it is time to depart.

TAURUS CHILD AND DIVORCE

The departure of a parent from the nest can be an upsetting experience for the little Bull, whose possessive instinct is strong and encompasses not only the favourite teddy bear but the entire family. If the child is under eight, it is best if the idea of mother or father not being around too often is instilled gradually — i.e. Daddy is very busy and won't be home so often now. This will allow the child time to become used to seeing him maybe only once a week. Young Taurus may not like it but in time will adapt. The first occasion that Daddy is not there when the child desperately needs him will lead to feelings of betrayal and an almighty scene may follow; it will be quickly learned that this works both ways and the child may become unreceptive the next time the erring parent visits. Over a period of months he or she will get used to being self-reliant or going to the remaining parent, and the missing parent will become a pleasant visitor. If divorce is necessary then as far as this little character is concerned it should be a clean break — no trial reconciliations followed by yet another parting, so the parents should not split in the first place until they are absolutely sure that it is over. The rule for the missing parent should be: either visit regularly or disappear completely; it is the kindest service you can do for this child.

The older Bull is even more of a problem. How dare you leave your own flesh and blood? No matter how tough the visits for the missing parent, they should refuse to rise to this bait and are advised simply to be there. After a while, probably a long while, the child will understand that this is the way it must be but won't be above trying to reconcile the parents. So prepare for some devious moods. As with anything new, the Bull needs time to adjust and cannot be hurried.

TAURUS CHILD AND REMARRIAGE

This is not an easy situation in which to find yourself. But who said that life had to be easy? If the child is over-friendly and loving with the new parent, watch out: trouble is in store. It may be that the new parent is seen as an opportunity for hitting back at the absent parent. However, at least this frame of mind will make it easier for you to get to know the child. With any luck, after starting out pretending to adore you, before the child realizes it, it may actually happen. If he or she suddenly becomes impossible without any obvious reason, then you will know you've really hit home, for the child is reproaching himself or herself for betraying the real parent. Keep calm. Let things ride and don't apply pressure. One day this guilt will be overcome and you will be accepted one hundred per cent.

However if the Bull is older and has decided that no way is he or she going to like you, then surrender. This is a determined sign, not to mention a stubborn one. Don't expect the child to budge. Conversely, it should not always be you who makes the overtures. The Taurus child is no fool and understand that because you love his or her mother or father attempts at friendship are important for you. By the same token, the child realizes that no matter how badly he or she behaves, that same parent's love and devotion can be relied on. Don't compete. Let the child know that you would like to be close, but are not going to grovel in order to obtain approval. This way, you will at least gain respect. In no circumstances can one push a Bull, and anyone who insists on doing so is asking to be mashed into the ground. Let the child be your yard-stick. Give only what the child wants, and above all else don't try to buy love. Young Taurus will have already worked out what you are good for and if you allow it will take you contemptuously to the cleaners. Gain this child's respect and comradeship, and with any luck eventually the love will come along, but take it in that order.

CONCLUSION

In the previous pages, we have discussed the pros and cons of various human relationships, but which is the ideal one for you? The commune? Yes, provided you are happily married and secure in your relationship. Cohabitation? Possibly, if you enter the relationship with marriage as your ultimate goal. Bachelorhood? Maybe while you are waiting for the right person; certainly not as a permanent arrangement. The Bull may be highly sexed, but is not naturally a polygamist. Marriage? You have it. You may have experienced one matrimonial storm instigated by your love of routine and possessiveness, but that should not prevent you from trying again. The Bull needs the security of family life; it may have bored the pants off you sometimes, but you are not really able to think of a satisfactory alternative. Naturally enough, if you have just been through a divorce, then the idea won't exactly appeal and rightly so: no Bull should rush into marriage. You should enjoy yourself for a while and wait for that special someone. You are not the type to mistake infatuation for love, so relax. Neither is there any need for you to feel ashamed at your failed marriage. It was only a lapse of judgement, after all. Yes, even you can make mistakes though you loathe to admit it. You are not to blame if at twenty you fell for a big pair of blue eyes which later you discovered belonged to a nymphomaniac, a sadist or a habitual gambler; just as long as you tried everything before throwing in the sponge. Of course, if you left because she used the wrong perfume or he forgot your birthday, then that is a matter between you and your conscience, although Taureans do not normally give up over such trivia. And if you were the one left, then maybe you could have been a little sweeter but he is already whispering sweet nothings into some blonde's ear or she has been carried off by the equivalent of Batman or Steve Austin. Then the resigned attitude will be the best way to go.

Besides, you surely don't think that you could forget all of those recriminations, the broken trust and start again, do you? You are a practical individual, so don't you forget it! In four years time when you are happily remarried, in or out of the commune, you will wonder why you ever thought that ex of yours was anything other than Dracula or his bride.

TAURUS MARRIAGE CHANCES QUIZ

Answer the questions honestly below and score 3 for yes, 2 for sometimes or unsure, and 1 for no.

1. Do you believe that a woman's place is in the home?
2. Do you think that looking after the kids is a woman's natural talent?
3. Are you possessive? (Ask your mate.)
4. Are you stubborn?
5. Is marriage for life?
6. Would it be impossible for you to take back an unfaithful spouse?
7. Are you against divorce?
8. Do you believe that mutual needs are more important than love?
9. Do children cement a marriage in your view?
10. Does it take a while for you to recover from a love affair?
11. Does your mate always remember your birthday?
12. Do you remember his/hers?
13. Do you find socializing a bit of a bore?
14. Would you miss your lover if you were separated for two days?
15. Do you believe that lovers belong to each other?
16. Do you tend to slip into a sexual routine?
17. Do you think it is impossible to love without feeling pangs of jealousy?
18. Are you proud of your mate's cooking or handywork in the home?
19. Do you hate debts?
20. Do you need to adhere to a budget?

ANSWERS

1 — 30: You may have your Sun in Taurus, but you must have several planets in Leo, Aries or Sagittarius. You take a light-hearted approach to relationships and dislike being restricted in any way. You will either avoid marriage altogether or go through anything up to five divorces. Needless to say, you are not ideal marriage material.

31 — 50: You are a typical Taurean and one with more virtues than vices. If you can't make marriage work, no one can. The marriage state can only benefit you, not just emotionally and sexually but also professionally. A happy background leaves you free to chase your ambitions.

51 — 60: You are a true Taurean, perhaps too much so, for you possess more of the faults than the virtues. You will never desert a husband or wife, but that is not to say they won't desert you, for you could well drive partners away by the demands you make. There is no doubt that you are a difficult one to live with. It is possible that unless you can be more adaptable, you will divorce several times.

GEMINI
(the Twins)
May 22 — June 21

Planet: Mercury
Colour: Yellow
Partners: (In general) Libra, Aquarius
Countries: Sardinia, Wales, Belgium, U.S.A.
Cities: London, Bruges, Metz, Melbourne, Plymouth, Cardiff
Famous Geminians: Judy Garland, Marilyn Monroe, Prince Philip, Richard Wagner, John F. Kennedy, John Wayne, Dean Martin, Bob Hope, Paul McCartney, Sir Laurence Olivier

GENERAL CHARACTERISTICS

The Geminian is intellectual and many-sided. Your forces go into brain and nerve, not heart, and you have a very sensitive, highly-strung disposition. Because of this, you need plenty of fresh air, rest and exercise. Your health is not robust, and there is a danger of nervous complaints if you are not careful.

You have a fine mind and an excellent memory, but unless they are kept away from stress and strain, they can deteriorate into confused thinking. You are intuitive and receptive, capable of expressing in speech and writing a continual stream of ideas, and very adept at argument. Geminians have the most versatile sign of the Zodiac, and you like variety in every facet of your existence. You are never so happy as when you are leading a double life. You are likely to have dual professions or two or more romantic interests at once. You often have several hobbies or other interests or diversions in your spare time.

In negative types, this bent can degenerate into a tendency to spread yourself too thinly, to do a lot of things haphazardly and nothing especially well. You fritter your time away frivolously instead of concentrating your energies sufficiently to achieve excellence or success. You may become distracted and restless, unable to stick to any regular or repetitious occupation for long.

The positive type of Geminian is, however, a reminder that this is a masculine sign. These people display much force and initiative. They are very definite in their views, have a range of talents and make excellent managers and executives. They are as firm and dependable as the negative type is irresolute and irresponsible.

Ordinarily, Geminians require more variety than other people. They need frequent vacations or holidays, and love to travel to many different places. They tend to work much more efficiently if there are changes in their schedules and breaks in their routines. They are adaptable to different people, situations and environments. The Geminian usually puts up with domesticity but does not participate wholeheartedly in family life. He may have a somewhat superficial attitude towards relationships with his relatives or spouse. He is ruled by the mind and, unless other influences are indicated on his birth chart to contradict this, his emotions are somewhat shallow. He tends to be a flirt, but this is a part of his nature and should not be taken seriously.

Gemini rules the hands and arms as well as the upper respiratory system, the nerves and the part of the brain controlling higher thought processes. You tend to be clever with your hands and like to use them constantly. You may well be a chain smoker, given your preoccupation with your lungs and hands.

You are very logical, but in an argument you may leave out a basic premise and come to conclusions that are therefore false. It takes a clever opponent to realize this, however, because the average person will be convinced by your rational remarks. Nevertheless, Geminians are quick thinkers and make excellent teachers, writers, news-papermen, public speakers and lawyers.

Most of your luck and success will come through intellectual pursuits. Patience is not your strong point. You are not very persistent, and you do not like routine work. You are, however, a true diplomat and adept at manipulating situations and people without antagonizing them. Apart from being extremely bright, you are also a rapid speaker, therefore, even though others may disagree with you, it is unlikely that they will actually have the opportunity to say so.

GEMINI AND MARRIAGE

A Geminian expresses love or devotion through the mind rather more often than the body. You are not over-fond of constant touching, which you may even describe as pawing. You incline to mental ideals rather than physical or domestic attractions. Your interest in love is easily aroused, though you have a short attention span, and you rarely actually seek concrete attachments. You may enjoy a romantic relationship with someone who physically attracts you, only to be abashed when you discover they have taken you seriously.

You are intellectual about love. You like to read about it and discuss it, but while you understand love, you rarely feel it. Your admirers come in pairs or larger numbers and you have a terrible time trying to decide which one to choose. Often you don't choose at all but simply enjoy the limelight. You would enjoy a harem, or the female equivalent. At times, one could justly describe you as frivolous.

Because of your love of change, boredom can be the greatest enemy to your relationships; it is difficult for one person continually to supply food for your intellect. Ideally, you should marry later in life; in this way, you may be able to restrict your tally of divorces to the singular. Your life tends to be full of multiples — and this can include marriage. You can find a million reasons for marriage, such as that it would further your career or that the companionship would be great, but when you discover that your partner has done little to enhance your prospects, or that perhaps the stimulating conversation has dried up, your intellect logically says it's time to go.

Conversely, as a Geminian motivated solely by love you fail to consider the practical side to life. You are a playful child and, for a while, a perfect delight. But when the big world insists on creeping into view, bringing with it money problems and the reminder of various duties to be performed, then you pout and refuse to play if life can't be lived on your own impractical terms. So you gather in your toys and resume the search for yet another playmate. Your attitude to sex hardly helps. You may for a while refrain from verbalizing your demands, but you do expect to be entertained, and if life sinks into a dull routine you lose all interest. You would rather read a good book than indulge in mediocre sex. You may well be emotionally motivated to marry in your teens, but chances are you will develop and grow away from your mate in a few short years. When mature and contemplating re-marriage, you are bound to be more sensible and get hitched for practical reasons, only to discover that you should have at least consulted your passions. So you flee — yet again. Third time around, with any luck, you may also consider the relationship from an emotional as well as practical viewpoint. If so, then number three could well be your lucky number. Otherwise it is on to number four, five, six ... stop! Can you go through life like this forever? You probably could, but in my own experience the Geminian either makes it the first or third time or not at all.

How can you help yourself? In the first place, try to find a partner who not only turns you on but whom you also find intellectually fascinating. Next fight that boredom syndrome, both in and out of bed. Instead of waiting to be entertained, don't you think it might be a good idea for you to provide the cabaret for once? You can, of course, continue with your feverish involvement in life, with the right partner who will want to join in, thus providing constant topics of discussion. And why not direct that active and intelligent head of yours to the physical side of your relationship? Invent ways to surprise and delight your mate; you will soon find that they will do likewise. Generosity and the ability to give are contagious, and eventually both will come quite naturally.

Things financial are a constant source of headache to you; but you must try to show an interest in this direction; maybe together with your mate you could use that splendid head of yours to conjure up ingenious ways of juggling the bills. Your harmless flirting won't do any serious harm either, unless it is taken to a heartless extent. "What flirting?" you ask indignantly. Well, even if you don't consider your interest in other people as flirtatious behaviour, I'm afraid your mate may. Don't get the idea that I am suggesting you should change. Not a bit of it! The rest of the human race needs the Geminian to keep them on their toes. Nevertheless, a more selfless attitude will assist you to find greater happiness, and that can't be bad, can it?

GEMINI HUSBAND

If you are looking for a man with a childish love of living, one whose mischievous boyishness will keep you alert and young, one who will respect your right to exist as an individual, then send in your application forms right now.

But hold everything. What's this document which appears to have been filled in by Mother Earth herself? I am afraid, little lady, you could be in for a bit of a shock. You are correct to assume that a Gemini husband will love your chocolate gateau, and that your efficiency around the home may incite him to write a poem to your virtues — if he has noticed, that is. And no doubt you will both enjoy charging through the house playing monsters with the kids — until the little darlings need a clean nappy, at which time he will be conspicuous by his absence. But how long do you suppose he can remain satisfied with domestic bliss? One year, two, three or maybe four?

Well, let us consider some of the problems. He will arrange for a baby-sitter, intending to whisk you away for the night and woo you all over again. Don't imagine he is going to understand when, in the midst of a poetic speech, you are up in order to ring the babysitter and check on the children? If you do, you are positively demanding to be disillusioned. All right, let's take his attitude to finances. The butcher, baker and candlestick-maker are all camped out on your lawn awaiting payment. What is his reaction? He deftly steps over them, one at a time, bidding them a cheerful good morning and trusting that their various businesses are thriving. He is in his car and halfway down the road before they have had a chance to catch their breath.

True, he may present you with a gift quite out of the blue, and that is sweet, isn't it? But please don't expect him to remember your anniversary or birthday. Now, let's be honest. You are the type who likes lots of lovely affection and physical love, but if you have a limited imagination, then you will need to prepare yourself for some lonely nights. No, my girl, you are just not this man's ideal soul mate.

Now who have we here? Miss Passion herself. Our Geminian subject really can't take all of your intensity, you know. Yes, of course, he loves you — he told you last month, didn't he? Why are you so insecure? Was his lunch companion attractive? Well, maybe, if you like that sort of thing ... And why does he leave work at such erratic times? Now you have got him stumped, he can't explain. Possibly he became engrossed with this or that problem and quite forgot to consider her soufflé in the oven. How thoughtless of him! Or perhaps he bumped into old so-and-so and simply started talking. You are never going to accept all of these lame excuses even though he is probably telling the truth; but let's be honest, you don't really like the idea of such a dizzy character leaving your side for one moment, do you?

In truth, the Gemini man's ideal is someone rather like himself, a lady preferably following her own career along similar lines to his own, too busy to notice what time he arrives home because she is rushing around like a maniac trying to get the fish fingers in the pan before he returns. It is quite possible, though, that this situation will be reversed, and that she will enter her love nest only to be greeted by the sight of this all male rushing around, red in the face, attempting to rescue some burnt offering from the oven. But what the hell? There is a take-away down the road and that will suffice for them. Are you beginning to get the picture? Providing the same girl is prepared to be seduced or seduce in the car, on the floor, in the bath or wherever takes their fancy, then possibly this man may settle down for life. But even so, don't rely on it too much.

GEMINI WIFE

Are you irresistibly drawn to the kind of girl who can't cook water without burning it? One who has difficulty even organizing the hot and cold taps at bath time? A female whose inquiring and insatiable mind is attracted to everything from the sex life of the praying-mantis to Kung Fu? Well, my friend, this is the only way to travel — take the magic carpet on the left, for here is the Geminian woman. But don't be in too much of a hurry. Consider before you leap aboard. Have you read the previous section on the Geminian husband? She is very similar, you know. Are you still interested? Then, great. Just one or two more questions. Do you expect the little woman to be content in the home? Are you determined to have hordes of children? And is your idea of living dangerously a quiet evening at home with her, participating in her excellent home cooking? What about your appearance — are you fussy about your wardrobe, liking your buttons to be firmly in place? And do you admire a woman who can work wonders with the housekeeping money? If you answered in the affirmative to any of these questions, then will you kindly leave this magic carpet immediately before you are bodily thrown off.

And what about you, sir? I see you are perusing this fine specimen. Tell me, are you the type of individual who is quite happy on arriving home, to roll up his sleeves and get stuck into cooking the dinner? You are? Good. Now, can you use your imagination between the sheets? Are you also happy to manage the purse strings and make some sense of the bills? Still not put off, eh? And do you like a female to be enigmatic, the type that other men openly admire? If you can honestly say yes to all of this, then climb aboard, you are just the man such a woman·needs. But do be warned. The Geminian is a child when it comes to being practical, though she will be delighted to work and contribute to the household budget, if you tell her how much is required of her.

There are other compensations. Her mischievous streak plus the ability to remain playful in the face of adversity will cheer you up no end when the boss gives you your marching orders. "Who wanted that silly old job anyway?" she gently murmurs, caressing your temples.

And what about motherhood? She will not shrink from changing the baby's nappy, but when you inspect her efforts it may be difficult for you not to be reminded of your first attempt at knots in the scouts. Nevertheless, your children will have a mother who does not recognize the generation gap, who will be a chum rather than a mum when an adolescent's heart is breaking over the first big romance. Babies, children and teenagers are all allowed as much consideration and time as an adult, and they respond accordingly. So, despite her faults, there is something to be said for the Geminian wife. Not much consolation, you may think, if you are the wrong man. But if you are still interested, then stick around.

GEMINI AND DIVORCE

Divorce is not exactly an unknown quantity to members of this sign. It is conceivable that, while entangled in the legal rigmarole and procedures, you may have thought that the world was about to come to an end. But when six months have elapsed I bet you have difficulty remembering the hearing at all. You are fortunate in having a built-in ability to forget whatever suits you. This is not a conscious action, it is simply your innate self-preservation coming to the rescue. Geminians can usually handle whatever life dishes out. Yes, you may be floored for a while — a split second more likely — but you automatically bounce back and emerge relatively unscarred, and at least, unlike the

Arietian, you do attempt to learn from past mistakes. However, in the main, the events leading up to the divorce are lost somewhere in the back of that active head.

There is one aspect to divorce which you find infuriating, and that is your difficulty in accepting the knowledge that you were unable to solve your problems. You take refuge in the fact that you were married to a dummy, a member of the opposite sex whose intellect was never located. It is a rare Geminian divorce which ends in bitter reproaches. As far as you are concerned the whole matter is closed. The relationship is dead, and that's it. You see no reason, however, to be on bad terms with your ex. You are the type who will keep in touch for years out of a friendly interest. During the months immediately after the divorce, you do not seriously consider re-marriage. Suddenly you are free and you place a high value on that freedom. The prospect of dating once more holds little appeal, and when you do, you will prefer safety in numbers. Dates with any one individual will be limited to two or three. You are not going to be trapped again. As time passes, you gather confidence and feel able to extricate yourself adeptly from any threatening restrictions. For an intelligent character, you are not too bright, are you? For once you reach this stage, you lower that guard, and then guess who becomes ensnared again? "Why not?" you protest. You have learned a heck of a lot about yourself and what you can give and take from another person. Great! Then you may make a success of number two. If not, no doubt you will eventually get around to number three, four, five. It's certainly one way of leading an eventful life, isn't it?

GEMINI EX-HUSBAND

The Gemini man makes a realistic candidate for perfect ex-hubby, with the possible exception of unreliability in connection with coughing up alimony or maintenance money. Not that you wish to avoid it (unless you are unemployed), but you do have the darnedest luck when it comes to catching the post, and you possess the irritating habit of disappearing for days at a time or being generally unobtainable when it comes to practical issues. But then this is one of the very reasons why you are an ex-husband. Providing we overlook this aspect of your personality, then you are a great ex. You are quite happy to take out that erring spouse of yours when she is feeling depressed. True, you might try to wheedle your way back into the matrimonial bed, but only if you receive adequate encouragement, otherwise you are happy to be on your way. You are content to be available when needed and equally content to disappear when a new romance enters her life.

You will even encourage her when it comes to adapting once more to a single existence, and won't mind in the least if you discover that she is in the throes of a heated affair with your closest friend.

Adaptable, that's the Geminian man. You are quick to realize that she has her own life to lead, and keep your fingers crossed that she will allow you the same privilege. You could be so darned understanding that she may have difficulty finding someone to match up with you. There will be times when you may consider re-marrying her. This I would advise against. While you and your spouse are separated you may well enjoy each other to the full, but this does not mean that you could be happy living together again. You may just not be compatible on the day-to-day level. Whenever you feel the impulse to consider this possibility, try recalling the reasons for the break-up in the first place; it will bring you back to your senses with a bump.

GEMINI EX-WIFE

There are certain problems which need to be solved before your value as an ex-wife can be appreciated. For example, while you were married, there was always someone to unravel those infernal bills, and you may be tempted to telephone that old spouse of yours in an effort to plunder his financial genius. It is recommended that initially he complies and helps you over this tricky patch, and once you have come to terms with the practical side to life, then your advantages as an ex-wife will shine forth. You may be left to bring up the children, but you are not the type to be a millstone round his neck every time Johnny needs a new pair of shoes. Somehow you will find a way to supply these shoes yourself. With new motivation and impetus going for you, you may even reach some pretty giddy heights career-wise, and you will not compensate for the gap in your life by seeking refuge in your children. Not for you the role of clinging mother living her life through them, though of course you adore them. Don't imagine you won't feel the occasional pang of bitterness, especially when your ex-spouse marches down the aisle with a nineteen-year-old Lolita. But your malice is shortlived. Geminians' moods rarely last longer than a couple of hours. Neither is it entirely out of the question that you will soon be offering advice on her new baby's feeding habits. Let's hope you will be too busy with a new love of your own, however.

Most ex-wives suddenly find themselves with time on their hands and, needless to say, this allows plenty of scope for recrimination. It is to your credit that you keep your hours filled to bursting point. "The past is dead, long live the present" is your motto. A word of warning, however: marriage on the rebound should be avoided if possible. You love communication with other people, and there will be occasions when you miss someone to debate and discuss the world's problems with. It is this kind of thing which can send you heading for the altar again long before you are ready for it, so force yourself to take time out in order to get to know yourself once more. Don't lose sight of the fact that you now have freedom. Surely it is worth hanging on to for a while? You certainly won't be short of admirers. It is an unusual

Geminian women who needs actually to look around for a man. Bear
in mind that while most men are attracted to you, there are very few
that you can actually live with in harmony.

GEMINI AND COHABITATION

There will be many occasions in life when this arrangement will be
ideal for the Geminian. One: when you are sailing along on cloud nine
and wish to discover whether or not you could make a go of marriage
with your new love. Two: when you get to the stage of feeling that you
know the wedding service by heart and really could not face yet
another march down the aisle.

But apart from these exceptions, cohabitation could lead to a
complicated life. There may be someone you are crazy about, but if
you are typical of your sign, you will soon find it difficult to resist the
charms of another dishy member of the opposite sex. Then life could
become very awkward if you have someone in the background to
whom you must report your movements. If you are to lead a happy
life, then you should either be married, emotionally involved, or not.
There cannot be a happy medium for you. Some people may be able
to live with one partner for six months and, with the conclusion of this
affair, set up home with someone else; and they may even enjoy their
six months of bliss. But loyalty does not come easily to you, and there
is no point in continually putting yourself in the position where this
failing will be abundantly clear. You need room for manoeuvre. It is
difficult enough for you to remember which one of the many you are
supposed to be dating that night without the added complication of
needing to invent lies for the benefit of a well-established love who is
watching your every move.

Now let's assume that you have marriage in mind. In these
circumstances, you are a pleasure to live with. You will put your heart
and soul into the relationship. Nevertheless, you will expect equal
response from your lover, and if after a period of time — say four or
five months — you feel that the relationship is becoming a little too
one-sided, then you will make a speedy exit. When this occurs, it is not
unusual for your abandoned lover to feel that they have sadly missed
out, in which case, belated overtures will come in your direction,
usually to no avail. Once the Geminian leaves, he or she is not about
to repent or return.

GEMINI AND THE COMMUNE

Whenever a member of this sign decides to adopt this way of life, you
can bet the move was stimulated by curiosity. Geminians are
uncomfortable with anything they can't understand. Conversely they
certainly would not dream of condemning it without at least giving it a
whirl first-hand. A commune could just be one of a million things
which at some point has captured their imagination. Because of this,
members of the commune will not long have the pleasure of the

Geminian's company, for, curiosity satisfied, he or she will be off probing into something else. Not that they wouldn't slot admirably into the community — on the contrary. Adaptability and intelligence would make a member of this sign a valuable asset, able to suggest a thousand improvements or point out exactly where everyone is going wrong in moments of confusion. But boredom would not let the Geminian stick around any longer than it took to check out the scene. Could Geminians be happy with this lifestyle? Yes, as long as it were possible to drop it and assume it again as fancy dictated.

GEMINI LOVER — MALE

Get out your Gemini-proof vest. This character will play havoc with those heartstrings. He is teasing, playful and flirtatious, and he is yours — or is he? "I love you, I want you, I'm yours," his doting companion states. He smiles smugly. "Be mine," she begs. Did you see him flinch? He gives out with a stunning smile. "What about some coffee?" is his reply.

On a practical level, he is only too happy to contribute to the bills or at least half of them. He will even participate in his share of the household chores. No doubt he can knock out a quick omelette every bit as efficiently as she can. But he will always remain elusive. At best, this has to be accepted. A word of encouragement: if he has been faithful to any girl for over a year, then wedding bells could be just round the corner. But has he? Is she really sure she has not been so dazzled by his twinkling eyes as to ignore what's going on behind them? Well, if she is not self-deceived, then possibly she has made it, for this man rarely confines himself to one female unless he is very heavily involved. Why should he when he can just as easily manage, two, three or more? Any lady who wants to keep this character needs to ensure that she is well up on all his interests, especially the current ones. That way he will be pleased to take her along to the local exhibition on Japanese torture instruments or whatever. But he will want to discuss them with her when they return and it won't take long for him to realize if she is faking. Another word of advice: she should never criticize his friends. He has no intention of giving them up, but he will see them when on his own,

The Geminian man follows his own will, and it is a tough job keeping up with such a character; but if a woman manages it, he will appreciate her efforts and hang on to her. After all, who else is going to put up with him?

GEMINI LOVER — FEMALE

If you are entering into a trial marriage with this lady, be careful that the marriage side is played unobtrusively. Domesticity to her is sitting at her lover's feet, staring into a big open fire on a winter night. It is waking in his arms in the morning, sharing food experimentation in the kitchen, decorating the bedroom in the middle of the night for the third time in as many months. What it is not is saving for a house, sitting in separate chairs in front of the television all evening, staying at home while he goes out with the boys, sex in the missionary position every Saturday night. Of course, the above can always be brought into play if you wish to ditch her, but it certainly will not lead to marriage.

But let's not be too derogatory. She does have assets. She is well-groomed and feminine, the type men like to admire. Sexually she is totally unpredictable; she will seduce you over the breakfast table, but when you decide to reciprocate at dinner time, she will act shocked, make a dramatic exit and leave you totally abashed. There is no particular pattern, so don't look for one. She is a siren one hour and as pure as the Virgin Mary the next, but at least she can guarantee you will never be bored, nor will you ever lose your sense of humour. She will smile understandingly if you decide to back some broken-down nag rather than pay the telephone bill. She will even forgive you if you forget her birthday. But fail to react and adapt to her many moods, take her for granted or refuse to confide in her and you will be in hot water.

Providing you like a challenge and a life fraught with uncertainty, then here is a girl for you; but don't keep her waiting for marriage over-long, if this is your arrangement. She is impatient, and if you don't want the goods, then she will wish to resume her search in order to find someone who does.

GEMINI CHILD AND DIVORCE

A Gemini child accepts divorce far more easily than children of other signs. Such an active character may not even notice that one parent is not around any more, until it is pointed out. However, that intelligence needs to be paid the highest respect. The plain truth is the order of the day in this case, at any rate for a Geminian child over the age of comprehension, and that varies greatly. Devotion to both parents does not mean this child wants them around his or her neck all the time, any more than you want your child's presence twenty-four hours a day. The biggest problems will arise with teenagers. Bear in mind that young Gemini is devious and adept at playing one parent against another for material gain. You will need to make it clear that the game must be played by your rules. Don't be afraid to put your foot down. Your child will respect this and with a shrug figure that it was worth a try anyway.

There is one big "don't" and that is never to introduce too many uncles and aunties. Young Geminians may appear vaguely amused but will reach the conclusion that you are desperately lonely and that it is their fault and, as each affair comes to a halt, may eventually decide that you must be a bit of a dead loss for not being able to hang on to anybody. If you want to maintain this youngster's respect, keep the lovers out of sight until the relationship reaches the point where he or she must be involved.

REMARRIAGE AND THE GEMINI CHILD

Here again the notorious Geminian adaptability comes into play; the little fellow can accept the remarriage as easily as the divorce, but the new parent will need to keep his or her wits sharp. Forget the toys intended as a bribe, postpone the trip to a football match, for a while anyway. Try to be a mystery to appeal to the child's curiosity. Reveal information about yourself gradually and only open up and relate all in exchange for equivalent information; for example: "I used to loathe school, got kicked out twice. How about you?" This way you will get to know each other on a deeper level. A word of warning, though: never try to deceive this child about yourself; the Geminian is not above doing a bit of detective work, and if you are caught out, you've had it. Nor is it a good idea to be too physically demonstrative, as caresses are often considered to be pawing — not something to see a new parent indulging in. But romping around, that's different. That's fun and games, and if there's anything a Geminian loves it's a chance to play. Be uninhibited. Don't worry about appearing to be a darned fool. A parent who can shin up a tree is far preferable to one who can help with homework.

The first time you, the new parent, are approached with a problem will be an indication that the verdict is that you aren't quite such a silly old fool, and then you will know you are actually getting somewhere. The Gemini child is a likeable individual and providing you exercise some common sense your problems will be minimal.

CONCLUSION

Geminians have more choice in relationships than other signs. Well, let's face it, you fit into practically any situation, don't you? In a commune, for example, as long as you are free to come and go with impunity. Bachelorhood? Again yes; in fact, if you have no desire to become a parent, this is probably the best lifestyle for you — and consider all the alimony and heartache you may be saving yourself. You'll be free to chase a hundred quarries if you so desire, and no doubt you will, with no one behind you telling you what to do. So this is a definite possibility, if a somewhat lonely one. Cohabitation is possibly only advisable if marriage is to be the end product. You do not make a loyal lover and will spend far too much time inventing excuses for not being where you should be. But if it is a trial marriage, then go ahead. That brings us to the last alternative, marriage itself. Yet again the answer is in the affirmative, but be prepared for several. You are not made of true Darby-and-Joan material so you had better accept it. You may, of course be the exception to the rule, but don't bet on it. You may go through two, three, even four, before finding someone able to adjust to your erratic personality, though then it will all have been worth it. However, I would recommend that you control your maternal/paternal instincts, for life could become rather confusing if your offspring are to have different mothers or fathers — but then again you like complexity, don't you?

As a Geminian you are an intelligent character who doesn't need me to tell you what is good for you. My remarks are aimed more at the die-hard, incorrigible type. If for example you have many planets in Taurus this will increase your chances of matrimonial bliss. I merely suggest that you refrain from guilt or shock if, before you know where you are, you find yourself with two marriages to your credit. Believe me, your sign is notorious for multiple marriages and lives. But if you can learn something from each experience and come out a little wiser, then this is hardly a failure, merely life.

GEMINI MARRIAGE CHANCES QUIZ

Answer honestly the questions below and score 3 for yes, 2 for sometimes or unsure, and 1 for no.

1. It is impossible for you to satisfy all sides to your character with one person?
2. Do you feel you are lacking in maternal/paternal instinct?
3. Do you prefer a flat to a house?
4. Are you flirtatious? (Ask your mate.)
5. Do you find a challenge irresistible?
6. Once you have a person or a possession, do you lose interest?
7. Are you quick-witted?
8. Can you manage two/three admirers effortlessly?
9. Is divorce simply unfortunate and nothing more in your view?
10. Would it be hard for you to live in an unmarried state with your man/woman?
11. Do you dislike jealousy?
12. Are you independent?
13. Do you need the excitement of a chase?
14. Do you find routine sex a drag?
15. Are you hopelessly impractical?
16. Do money problems bore you?
17. Do you like to be the dominant partner in a relationship?
18. Are you absent-minded?
19. Do you enjoy quizzes such as this one?
20. Are you outspoken?

ANSWERS

1 — 30: You are too consistent and domesticated to be a true Geminian; you must have several planets in Cancer, Pisces or Taurus. But don't worry, this increases your chances of eventually playing Darby to someone else's Joan. A divorce would be difficult for you to cope with, and therefore you will fight to keep your marriage stable.

31 — 50: You are a typical Geminian, and while you may go through at least one divorce it won't take its toll on you, neither will it disillusion you. With your optimism, you must eventually find that soul-mate, even if you do leave a string of broken hearts along the way.

51 — 60: This is the score of a Geminian in possession of more than his fair share of this sign's faults. You leap in and out of marriage far too easily and unless you can learn from your past and be more discriminating in the future, it won't be long before you break Henry VIII's record of six spouses.

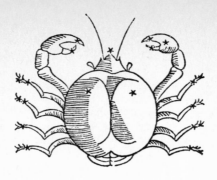

CANCER
(the Crab)

June 22 — July 22

Planet: The Moon
Colours: Violet and Silver
Partners: (In general) Scorpio and Pisces
Countries: Scotland, Holland, Paraquay
Cities: Amsterdam, Istanbul, Milan, Venice, York, St Andrews
Famous Cancerians: Phyllis Diller, Ernest Hemingway, Leslie Caron, Ringo Starr, Steve Lawrence, John Glenn, Paul Anka, Helen Keller, Arthur Ashe, Rembrandt

GENERAL CHARACTERISTICS

There is more difference between active and passive types in Cancer than in any other sign. The active type is strong-willed and very persistent. Natives of this water sign have as corrosive an effect on anything they set out to change or destroy as the milling waters that eat away an ocean cliff. These people are masterful in their approach to life and tirelessly active. Usually, they are very up to date and are interested in everything modern and current. The passive type, on the other hand, is contented, lackadaisical and idle, with little desire to make the effort necessary for accomplishment. He or she takes the line of least resistance, come what may, but is very tenacious and clings to what is already possessed. Both types are the product of their environment and are very much influenced by early training. You are usually very much attached to your home and mother. You absorb ideas and sense impressions from the world around you and, after digesting them, convert them to a new use. You are active in this way even though you may not be physically active.

You usually have an easy-going disposition and are faithful in love, a combination that makes for happiness in marriage. You are very sensitive, however, and can be deeply hurt by unkind criticism. You feel very sorry for yourself when you do not get your own way, and if this happens often you may take a kind of perverse pleasure in a martyr complex. You are extremely sentimental about the past and rarely discard old ties and friendships, even when you have long outgrown them. You like all sorts of antiques, old books and art objects, and when these have historical interest, you can become an avid collector. You have a real knowledge of history; if your interest is mainly personal, of your own genealogy and the affairs of your relatives and friends or of some special period or periods of the general historical past. You are especially fond of anecdotes and love to reminisce.

Your interests are very domestic. If a woman, you are a devoted homemaker and mother. If a man, you like to help around the house and be mothered by your wife. You are especially interested in what goes on in the kitchen and may even cook yourself. This often results in an unwholesome appetite and love of rich food and sweets. Cancerians are also likely to over-indulge in alcohol. Cancer rules the stomach, the breasts and lower lungs, and you are likely to suffer from these parts, also indigestion, ulcers and other digestive disorders. You are very emotional and you respond to love, approval and sympathy. You like the adulation of the crowd and to feel popular. For this reason, even if you are only an amateur, you love to act. You like to receive publicity and may also like the theatre or, more commonly, television.

You possess a sixth sense and your intuition is unbeatable. You can be sure of something without exactly knowing how you know. You may, however, be somewhat passive mentally. Only when someone argues with you do you resent it. An appeal to the senses and not logic influences you. You love to refer to the past, and your answer to a present-day problem is to quote a precedent from antiquity rather than dealing with the circumstances at hand — often a mistake, unless you intend to become a lawyer when this characteristic would be an asset, for you would rest your case primarily on research rather than relying on reasoning powers and more aggressive traits of mind. You are very sensitive to other people and to your surroundings. Yet while you are kind and very sympathetic, you cannot tolerate being with uncongenial people. This is not a particularly good placing for mental vigour, for the mind tends to be inactive and overly impressionable.

CANCER AND MARRIAGE

Love is a prime requirement for you. In fact, you need an emotional outlet for your health and general well-being. However, while you tend to be passive in matters of affection, you are always emotional. You rarely go hunting for love; you wait until it comes to you. And when someone pursues you, you accept their attentions gratefully because you find it difficult to resist the advances of a suitor. Your feelings are deep and quiet. You are intensely sentimental and need strong family ties. Although you take love seriously, you get over disappointments easily. A lonely Cancerian is a sorry sight. You are not meant to live alone. There must be someone for you to worry about and fuss over. The swinging bachelor was certainly not born under this sign.

Cancerians marry early in life in order to establish a family of their own. You only function normally when part of the family unit, preferably the most important part. However, you need to learn that domesticity is only part of marriage, not its reason for existence. Failure to recognize this fact is why many Cancerian marriages end in the divorce courts. No one can fault your cooking or your promptness at attending to chores and surely only another Cancerian could make a floor shine like you. Your garden probably deserves a place in the best glossy magazine. Furthermore, who would deny that you are an excellent parent who is able to handle the kids wisely without even an issue of discipline. And maybe, if your spouse is equally as domesticated, then you may live forever in an insulated self-made cocoon.

But frankly, there are those who would be nauseated at the very thought of such routine. Consider for a moment that there are plenty of people who not only enjoy their home lives but are also involved in what is happening in the big outside world. There are still yet others who would prefer to get their teeth, perhaps lustfully, into your soft flesh rather than your most exquisite apple pie. And there are even other members of the human race who spend more time at the office striving to achieve their ambitions than they do at home. Yes, the world is full of different people. Make sure you marry someone who needs and wants the same things as you do, otherwise you are heading for a good deal of trouble and heartache.

Until now that old devil sex has been ignored, but this simply won't do. Physical love to you is just an act of gentle devotion, and why not? But let's try being realistic. This could be likened to eating beef for breakfast, lunch and dinner, seven days a week. It is strange how you, as a crab, will go to unbelievable lengths in order to cook a meal, yet expect your spouse to be happy with the same sexual menu week after week after week. You should learn that if two people love each other, nothing they do together is wrong or disgusting. Love is changeable, it has different moods, and needs different ways of satisfaction. Your mate may want to be playful, basic, ridiculous or experimental. The main point is he or she wants all of this with you, not the attractive type down the road. Although if you fail to respond for long enough, then he or she may well call in the first reserve.

Yes, versatility and an awareness of what is happening in the world could go a long way to making you the perfect spouse.

CANCERIAN HUSBAND

Ladies, pay attention. The label on this lot reads: "The Cancerian Husband". It further states that he is sympathetic, practical and devoted to those he loves. He is also credited with being extremely imaginative and sensitive. Now what offers do I hear? Yes, Miss, you are prepared to extend a life contract plus a substantial sum from your impressive salary? I see, a career lady, are we? Well, let's talk about it. Are you prepared to ask for a reduction in hours to enable you to tend efficiently to this man's needs? And that means rushing back at nights in order to do the shopping, clean the house and cook a meal before he arrives home. You are not? I suspected as much. And how do you feel about four or five children whose needs will invariably be placed above your own? Suddenly you are struck dumb, madam. Well, do you make an efficient nurse? Can you rush around with an air of doom as though attending to a patient with pneumonia, when all he is suffering from is an attack of indigestion or possibly a hangover? And lastly, how are you at ego-building? Can you sweep away insecurities that strike at four in the morning? Miss, I said can you ... Where are you? Well, perhaps it's for the best. Frankly, that kind of woman just isn't the Cancerian man's type anyway.

Right then, here we go again. The subject is once more ready to consider any reasonable offers. Yes, lady ... you think he has possibilities and could be changed perhaps more to your liking? Well, maybe he could adjust but only a fraction, and I shouldn't rely on it if I were you. You have been around, a bit of a girl about town, would you say? Let me suggest, Miss, that you reconsider. Are you prepared to throw away that address book, keeping only in touch with three or four close friends? And do you think you could adapt to a cosy evening at home with friends, partaking perhaps of some excellent home cooking created with your own fair hands of course? Swish restaurants are strictly out, I'm afraid, so too are expensive night-clubs and discos. The Cancerian loathes superficial surroundings and can hardly tell a waltz from a shake. Neither is he that keen on females who dress like fashion plates. He prefers a woman to be clean, neat, pretty, but comfortable. Yes, lady, you are right, there is no point in continuing and I'm glad you recognize the folly of your offer.

Back to the drawing-board, young ladies, he is still available. And who is this I can see sitting demurely at the back of the auditorium? Well, it's Miss Homemaker herself. You would be happy to devote yourself to our friend, wouldn't you? Your individuality would not be worth anything without the right man, am I correct? Yes, I thought so. And how you do love those fluffy pink-cheeked babies. What about your cooking? You took an evening course at the local institute, you are a Cordon Bleu? I can't say I am surprised. Furthermore, I bet you made that natty little creation you are wearing. There's a clever girl! Right, ladies, that's it. Our Cancerian man has been taken by the pretty little lady on the left. It is time to shut up shop. Try your luck next time.

CANCERIAN WIFE

Do you admire a girl with ambition? That female who is capable of paying her own bills and taking her own decisions? If you do, then the Cancerian lady is not for you.

And what about you, sir? You look as though you are in need of care and attention. You are the type who makes the sewing on of a button or the boiling of an egg seem as impossible as flying to Pluto. You are also attracted to the idea of having a woman to attend to your every whim. Yes? I thought so. And no doubt that you would be prepared to have a million children, provided that she kept them out of your way. I see that I am correct. Well, sensitive, home-loving and sweetly domesticated though the Cancerian lady may be, that does not mean you can drive a truck through one of her ears and out of the other, so kindly leave this section before it explodes in your face.

What this woman requires is a partner, not a slave-driver. She wants a man who will take an active interest in the building of their nest. A handy man or a do-it-yourself enthusiast would be ideal. He needs to be a good father, and that means more than just the paying of a few bills. Furthermore, she would expect her man to be competent enough to stumble through the domestic routine should she be incapacitated — not that she suffers from ill-health, you understand, but she will fall victim to the occasional psychosomatic ailment whenever she is depressed or believes herself to be generally ill used. What's that you say, sir? You are still interested, and you have a bottomless well of love for the right woman. Great! Then she is all yours. The two of you should be blissfully happy.

CANCER AND DIVORCE

Even the word divorce is enough to send the average Cancer running for cover under the nearest rock. A broken marriage hits both the male and female of this sign sideways. The crab clings to ideas, possession and people. When the spouse escapes, you can bet it is metaphorically necessary to take the Crab's claw on departure. The Cancerian always prefers to lose an arm rather than let go. When this sign is involved in divorce the whole affair often becomes rather sordid, petty and bitter. Needless to say, such a state of affairs should be avoided in the first place. It is essential that marriage be undertaken only when both parties are very sure of their chances of survival. The term "gay divorcee", is not applicable to this sign. A lone Crab is a pathetic sight; that admirable, soft centre is submerged beneath a thick tough shell, and once this occurs, it is practically impossible for anyone or anything to make even the slightest dent. Not surprisingly, then, re-marriage is frequently rejected. The risk of yet another failure is too great, and not one the average Crab is prepared to take.

Should divorce be inevitable, then try to prepare yourself for the experience. First you should tell yourself you have done nothing to be ashamed of, and to hell with the neighbours — they will have another character to assassinate next week. And what about those friends? If they are going to drop you because of a divorce, then honestly, aren't you best rid of them? Forget about other people, including your erring spouse. Think about your future. Slipping into self-pity won't achieve anything, life goes on. Now what about the character who deserted you? Well, you may get them back by being understanding or even indifferent, but an embittered martyr anyone would be glad to be free of. Make immediate plans; brooding over the past is the worst thing you can do.

Though divorce is hell for the Cancerian, an embittered reconciliation takes an even greater toll. Look on the demise of your marriage as a cure for a sick and ailing relationship and, above all else, forget the recriminations.

CANCERIAN EX-HUSBAND

The tendency of the Crab to hang on has repeatedly been referred to, and yet it is necessary to mention it again. For even when the decree absolute is granted and filed, this does not necessarily mean that his emotions can also be conveniently shelved, despite the fact that he may have been the one to leave. Inner conflict is increased if children are with the ex, and any subsequent lover will have to accept the fact that the Crab will occasionally suddenly disappear in order to satisfy an unexpected paternal/maternal urge to see the children.

Financially speaking, he is a gem. He pays up on the button and with the exact amount — not a fraction over or under. However, later when she tries to spread her wings and actually starts dating again ... oh, dear! He is a nervous wreck. For no matter how diabolical she may have been as a wife, he still believes she belongs to him, no court can alter that. Only she can bring him to his senses but it takes time. Much depends on her psychological makeup. If she is a sensitive type, she is in trouble. Every time he is depressed or has had a fight with his girlfriend he will arrive looking for a shoulder to cry on, and sometimes a good deal more. And if his ex-wife permits it, he will use her on the slightest pretext and she could well be hooked for life. The soft-centred woman invariably tells herself that one day he will return, but he never will, not for more than a night anyway.

One needs to be firm with the Cancerian. He can visit the children as arranged and be invited also on special occasions, but that's it. The first time he telephones in the middle of the night, or turns up without regard for her privacy, she must act decisively; he must be taught to recognize the fact that they are now two separate entities, whether he likes it or not. And if he ignores her protestations, then it may become necessary to enlist the help of the court or a big-shouldered boyfriend. This little game must be squashed before it begins, otherwise there is no hope for either of them or their new loves. Yes, as an ex-husband, the Cancerian would make a better statesman.

CANCERIAN EX-WIFE

If there is anything more impossible than an ex-Cancerian husband, it is an ex-Cancerian wife or two Cancerian ex-wives, etc. ... This female is a walking example of the "working my fingers to the bone" syndrome, or "He has had the best years of my life". There is not much you can do with a woman who is determined to be a martyr, except fix her up with a new love. Matters may be improved if she was the one to desert. There is nothing like a liberal dose of guilt to shut her up; otherwise be prepared to have every cent or penny you earn painfully extracted. Stay calm when she tracks down your latest love and treats her to tales of your brutality. You can, of course, gulp down a tranquillizer when she demands you visit her at eleven at night because Johnny has toothache or she is about to slash her wrists. But wouldn't it be easier to move away as far as you can? Two thousand miles should be a nice, safe distance.

"Unfair, unjust, untrue!" I hear the Cancerian lady cry. Well, ask yourself: isn't there quite a lot of truth in these statements? I hope I am wrong. What you should be doing is looking to the future or at least the present. Take a look in the mirror. What size were those hips when your erring spouse first swept you off your feet? Size 8. And what are you now, since you have been sitting around gorging yourself on doughnuts or some such sweetmeat, hating all men and planning retribution? Enough, I say. Get a new hairstyle, start a new wardrobe in the size you realistically hope to achieve. Join a health club, give a party and find yourself a date or let a friend do it for you. You have to adjust to your new-found freedom, give it a chance. After all, be honest. Was that ex of yours such a fine catch? Are you seriously suggesting that you can't find anyone better? Of course not. Half the world's population are men, there must be at least one who is perfect for you, but you will never know where he is if you just sit in every night watching the television, will you?

A positive attitude plus a well-aimed kick would do wonders for you and your imaginary problems. You are not as young as you used to be, but neither are any of the men you once used to date. So polish up that shell, throw away the bedside picture of your ex and start living once more.

CANCERIAN AND THE COMMUNE

Ridiculous, you might initially think, but consider the home-loving qualities of the Crab. Cancerians thrive on family responsibility.

Imagine how they would blossom under such conditions. She could teach all the women to cook, clean and sew, be a veritable guiding light, or he could knock up all kinds of beautiful constructions. These domesticated talents would make them a very important part of a commune, and the Cancerian adores the limelight. Yes, members of this sign could do a good deal worse than consider such a lifestyle. And what about the free advice which would be liberally doled out? The only problem could arise when some independent soul dared to tell the Cancerian exactly what they can do with their pearls of wisdom. But apart from this, the communal life should be relatively drama free.

THE CANCERIAN AND COHABITATION

The Crab is very conventional in personal relationships, so in normal circumstances this is not an arrangement that will attract. But the Cancerian is a sensitive soul, and easily influenced by experiences and other people, therefore, much depends on environment. The young Crab living in a busy metropolis and socializing in sophisticated circles may, upon observing and mixing with the so-called swinging set, decide that this is the way to go and after much soul-searching may take the plunge.

Another situation which may lead to cohabitation is divorce blues. The Crab may be too disenchanted with marriage ever to attempt it again. But what is the domestic Crab to do, needing a home and someone to share it with? For a while, this seems to be a solution. In most cases, however, this individual would be behaving true to character. For no matter how sophisticated or embittered Cancerians may believe themselves to be, the truth is that marriage is the ultimate goal for all those born under this sign and they are destined to be unhappy in their relationships until they get to know themselves and accept their limitations.

The only time cohabitation may work for them is as a trial marriage providing, of course, he or she is not kept waiting too long. The Cancerian is an insecure homemaker, and the sooner you recognize this fact the sooner you will find inner peace. Never place yourself in a vulnerable position: cohabitation without some kind of agreement is a self-destructive arrangement for you.

CANCERIAN LOVER — MALE

He may initially be the happiest man in the world and a delight to live with. After all, he has at last that much coveted home and a little woman ... or has he? And one day they will tie the knot won't they? And then everything will be perfect — or will it? Are you getting the picture? The Crab is notorious for his clinging, and when doubts and uncertainties begin to nag, he will hold on to his lover until she eventually has to fight herself free of him. It is a sad situation; at first she may be flattered by his need to be constantly at her side and the cute way he begs "Please never leave me," but gradually he begins to irritate and she starts to withdraw. This is counteracted by a "You mustn't ever leave me" plea, but when it reaches the "I KNOW you will leave me" stage, then enough is enough. He seems to possess a death wish when insecure, and before long his wish is granted. It had not entered her head that possibly they would split, but now — well, maybe he is right; perhaps, they aren't that happy and so it goes. He tightens his grip, she tries to extricate herself. In the end, of course, she is successful, even if it does mean exercising a heart-wrenching yank.

Poor old Crab, didn't he know it would happen? His intuitions are never wrong. He cannot understand that it is he who has brought the world crashing about his ears. Therefore, Mr Crab, if you must put yourself in this position, let me suggest an engagement. Yes, I know, they can be broken, just like marriages. But at least it may calm those niggling insecurities of yours for a while.

CANCERIAN LOVER — FEMALE
This lady is very much like her male counterpart. She delights in having her own home, even if it is only one room. She cleans it until she can see her face in everything, including the carpet. She sings to herself in the kitchen while attempting to surprise and delight his palate, and she is desperately hurt when her lover dares to hint that he did not really set up home with her so that she could slave away on it all the time. She needs to understand that encouragement when he is down or worried is better than a spotless floor. Interest and understanding of his job is more important than a soufflé that did not collapse. And love-making can be enjoyed at any time and in any room. Furthermore, for her own peace of mind, she should never kid herself that she can indefinitely live with anyone without the promise of marriage, if only because it's just a matter of time before her maternal instincts surface. Members of other signs may produce love children, but this female is far too conventional. Be true to yourself, sister Crab, and you will automatically shy away from those situations which are self-destructive to you.

CANCERIAN CHILD AND DIVORCE
Divorce is bad enough for mature Cancerians who can understand that they are partly to blame, but a child needs careful handling to escape being turned into a delinquent. This screwed-up youngster pushes sensitivity and love inside and displays only that hard outer shell, and if you think you are going to get through once this occurs, forget it. Ask anyone — mother, father or probation officer. When the news is given that a parent has departed, there may be no outward show of emotion — great if there is, but more likely the child will creep off alone somewhere with the heartache. If possible the present parent should follow and even in the face of reproachfulness try to make the youngster spill it out, for this is the healthiest way. After the

initial blow, it is up to the missing parent to reassure and establish exactly when visits will occur. Ideally they should be more frequent than is normal in divorce; there needs to be a definite pattern which must never vary, and eventually the Crab will accept the new routine. If for whatever reason these visits cannot take place say twice a week, then it may be far kinder for Daddy or Mummy to disappear completely overnight. Upsetting, yes, but having recovered from the shock the Cancerian child will at least know where he/she stands. It will then be up to the present parent to dole out large doses of love. It is a good idea to let the young Crab feel every bit as needed as he or she needs you and know that now you must help one another. By learning to think of you the child will not dwell so much on personal grievances or sink into a martyr complex.

CANCERIAN CHILD AND REMARRIAGE

Here again much depends on circumstances. If one of the natural parents is completely absent, then the notion of finally becoming part of what is considered a proper family may outweigh every other consideration. And as long as the new parent does not behave like King Kong or Cinderella's step-mother all will be well. The young Crab has enough love for two parents and in fact can be rather much for only one. It won't be long before the step-parent is totally accepted. However, life could be more difficult when the Cancerian child is in close contact with both natural parents. The trick here is never to expect to replace the absent parent in this youngster's affections. Rather try to demonstrate that the love of three parents must be better than that of two. And love is the key word. It doesn't matter how influential you may be, how big your car is, etc. ... only how big your heart is; and a new parent who in all honesty cannot grow to love this child should get out before everyone is hurt. Without a secure home, loving parents, the young Cancerian may grow into a dry-eyed, mixed-up adult. And the moment love is offered from outside the family, this child will worship blindly the stranger concerned — however unsuitable — and will eventually grow to be like them. Before you know where you are, your child will be the local hooker or thug. So get out that large bottle marked "love" and give daily doses — it is the only way.

CONCLUSION

Having discussed on the previous pages various relationships, we must now decide which is the ideal human relationship for the Crab.

First let's consider cohabitation. Not ideal for the reasons mentioned. It may work if marriage is the end product, but otherwise this is a self-destructive scene for the Cancerian, despite the argument: "Well, I have lived with four people successfully." But who are you kidding? If it was at all successful, then you would still be with number one.

A commune then? Yes, why not? Providing you enter this lifestyle with a willing partner, you are one of the few people who would delight in mucking in with other people. In fact, you would be an inspiration. How long you would stay is difficult to say; probably you would be the last to leave. It is easy to imagine you standing there whilst the others gradually move out one by one. Eventually, you would be extolling the virtues of your big, happy family to a large empty room. You could look pretty silly just standing there talking to yourself.

Now we come to marriage. This, of course, is tailor-made for you. You probably can't understand why some people find marriage too claustrophobic, too intense. However, do remember before entering this happy state, that you do not survive divorce easily and should therefore be more cautious than most.

Lastly we have bachelorhood which is not really your scene, for more than a few short months anyway. You would rather sow your oats in one familiar field, so find yourself a lover with the same priorities as yourself, and you should be able to make a bid for the Darby and Joan award of the year. Later in life, of course, marriage is never easy, but fortunately you understand this and are determined to make it work. Most of the time you succeed, but never lose sight of the fact that you may not be, for this will keep you on your toes. Good luck to you, my Cancerian friend; may you never find anyone who can irretrievably damage that hard shell.

CANCERIAN MARRIAGE CHANCES QUIZ
Answer these questions honestly and score 3 for yes, 2 for sometimes or unsure, and 1 for no.

1. Do you try to ensure that domestic impulses do not impose on your sex life?
2. Are you a good cook?
3. Are you at a loss on a dance floor?
4. Do you adore babies?
5. Do you feel uncomfortable in a room full of strangers?
6. Do you have a large appetite?
7. Do you regard your job as simply a way of surviving and nothing more?
8. Are you opposed to divorce?
9. Are you basically against sex without emotional commitment?
10. Is it difficult for you to recall reading a book during the last six months?
11. Have you been living at your present address longer than three years?
12. Do you enjoy bargain-hunting?
13. Do you loathe letter-writing?
14. Do you believe one hour's sleep before midnight is the

equivalent of two after?
15. Do you keep regular meal times?
16. Could you adopt a child?
17. Do you watch television at least three nights a week?
18. Do you suffer from any regular niggling ailment such as headaches, indigestion, nerves etc?
19. Do you need lots of affection?
20. Is the past very real to you?

ANSWERS

1 — 30: You are just not domesticated enough to be a true Cancerian. This together with the fact that you need a certain amount of freedom leads me to believe that you have several planets in Gemini, Sagittarius or Aquarius. Don't rush into marriage, for if you do it may well end in divorce.

31 — 50: This is the score of the true Cancerian. You possess more of the sign's virtues than the vices. Providing you can find someone who possesses a similar list of priorities, then you may make your diamond wedding anniversary. But try to widen your interests. It will help you to keep the monotony out of your marriage.

51 — 60: This is the score of the Cancerian with more of this sign's faults than its virtues. You may fervently believe that you will never experience divorce but you are just the type to drive your spouse straight up the wall and out of your life, with the humdrum way you like to live and your closed mind. No intelligent person could stay willingly or happily with you for long. There is the big world outside your front door, why not get out and see what it is all about? You could be sorry if you don't.

LEO
(the Lion)
July 23 — August 23

Planet: Sun
Colour: Orange
Partners: (In general) Aries and Sagittarius
Countries: Italy, France, Rumania
Cities: Chicago, Philadelphia, Los Angeles, Rome, Prague, Damascus
Famous Leonians: Jacqueline Onassis, Princess Margaret, Napoleon, Lucille Ball, Eddie Fisher, Fidel Castro, Princess Anne, Mick Jagger, Percy Bysshe Shelley

GENERAL CHARACTERISTICS

The Sun is your ruling planet and, because of this, you are proud, noble and magnanimous. You would not stoop to do anything mean or underhand, and you find it hard to believe ill of others. If and when they offend you, while you may retaliate swiftly, you forgive easily and never hold a grudge. Just as you trust others, so you want to be trusted absolutely. You will do anything to live up to the confidence that has been placed in you. You like to be responsible and in a position of authority, otherwise you will neglect your duties and fall down upon your work. You are a hard worker but you do not like menial tasks, you might perform a menial task as an example to others, or if there is no one else to do it, but you would not like it as a steady diet. You are bored by repetition and petty detail. You are strong, ambitious and masterful. You seem so ready for a fight that most people are wary of challenging you. Once you become involved in one, your tactics are fair and above board. You would not consider using deceit. Your courage may seem reckless to less honourable types. You have a great deal of self-confidence and a good opinion of yourself. But you require the adulation and approval of others. If you don't find this in the world at large you retreat into a smaller circle where yours is the brightest light. You definitely prefer to be a big fish in a little pond. If your ambitions outside the home are thwarted, you can react by turning into a domestic tyrant and lording it over your immediate family.

Sometimes you can be boastful; you tend to have the attitude that whatever is yours is best in the world and, as this is not always the case, you may incur the resentment of those who remain unconvinced. You need more affection than the average person and an emotional outlet is essential to you at all times. You love wholeheartedly and you give yourself unreservedly to your love. Because you are so convinced of your worth to others, you cannot conceive of being refused. Once you have sworn to love and protect, you tend to live up to your promises, no matter how unworthy the object of your affections may turn out to be.

You are very adventurous and can face any danger in the pursuit of your ideals. You are insatiably ambitious and no amount of success can content you, but you refuse to accept your limitations. Yes, you attempt the impossible and failure makes you very unhappy indeed. You have an unusually magnetic personality and, if possible, you should attend to important business in person, because your enthusiasm is contagious and you are better able to influence others that way. You are a wonderful host or hostess and you love to entertain.

Leo rules the heart and the back, and, though you have enormous vitality, great expenditure of energy can be too much strain on either should you be careless. Sight is your most developed sense but your other senses are healthy and normal. You must, however, have some interest in, and some affection for, the subjects before you can learn. The first appeal must be made to your heart rather than to your head. Once your emotions are aroused no one can learn faster or more accurately. What you believe is irrevocably linked with your affections, you have very little natural curiosity and only in rare cases do you have a scientific turn of mind. You are independent and love your freedom and you have a great deal of initiative and an optimistic approach to life. You make an inspired, capable leader with great vigour and self-reliance, and you may even feel that you have a mission to perform.

LEO AND MARRIAGE

In most kinds of personal relationships you are very popular. You simply naturally attract the warmest feelings from others. They are drawn to you because of your kindliness and heartfelt geniality. Even your worst enemies have nothing personal to say against you.

Although some people may not admire you, they have to like you because you are generally so big-hearted. Your willpower and magnetism are tied in with the dictates of your heart. You are very magnanimous with the world at large and your nobility and decency are always apparent. You are a great humanitarian. In your intimate relationships, with your family and those you love, you can be loyal beyond the call of duty. When you love, you are generous to a fault with your affections as well as with material possessions. Leo's fire may make you passionate but you are always demonstrative and warm. Whom you love depends on their appeal to your deeper emotions; you like to dominate those you love and part of your personal magnetism stems from your strong will-power. Still ... you are capable of great sacrifice for a worthy cause or for the happiness and welfare of your loved ones.

That's the good news, anyway. Now for the bad ...

Leonines, especially the men, tend to be quite conceited: not only are they impressed by their own importance, but by their mental and physical powers as well. They are often so egotistical that they do not take others' feelings and reactions into consideration at all, and are impervious to outside influences, when they should be taking them into account. This is not quite so true of the female Leo, who tends to be more modest in contrast to the male, and usually has a fine, well-balanced personality. But Leo indicates the full expression of the emotions and a terrific amount of drive. You are not only ardent in your affections but express yourself in an open, confident manner and with a certain amount of warmth of heart. You do things with a flourish and in the grand manner. When you speak or write you are eloquent and persuasive. Your appeal is from the heart and so is the response that you inspire. Napoleon was a typical example. His letters were not only eloquent and imaginative, but also fiercely passionate.

Because you are so warm and giving, one would automatically assume that marriage and Leo would be almost synonymous, but not so. One of your biggest faults is that you simply do not like to take, and therefore your generosity in close relationships is not only embarrassing but, perhaps more important, can lead to blocked communication lines. No matter how little we have to give, we all need the opportunity to do so, especially when in love. You are fond of flattery, another characteristic that can have an unfortunate effect on personal relationships, for you are not above choosing a partner less clever or fortunate than yourself, simply to make it easy for you to dominate or shine. You are going to be the King, or the Queen, as the case may be, and your partner had better not forget it! All very well, if you have chosen a soft and gentle soul, but what happens if your partner turns out to be as determined as yourself? H.G. Wells's *War of the Worlds* will give you some idea!

I realize that I have committed the unthinkable — no one in their right mind makes attempts at damaging the lion's ego, but fortunately I am at a safe distance! And besides, there is no need to sink into despair; you are quite capable of making a happy marriage, provided you have chosen a partner out of the best motives. Someone you can love and cherish and someone you will be happy to step down from your throne for. And someone with whom you can live on an equal footing in your everyday existence.

LEO HUSBAND

Gather round, ladies, and let's see what we have for you on view today. According to his card this fine specimen is the Leo husband ... Well, before we commence bidding, let me first tell you that this character is proud, generous, affectionate and egotistical. He has a penchant for beautiful and elegant women, and tends to wear the opposite sex rather in the same way he would a hand-made suit. Dear me, Miss, I'm afraid those flip-flop shoes and your denims would never do! You must understand that he needs to feel good, and an attractive wife gives his insatiable ego a boost. He won't mind if you are as dim as last year's Christmas tree lights, just as long as you are presentable. What's that you say? A male chauvinist pig? No, Madam, wrong animal. Lion perhaps, King of the Jungle given the chance, but never a pig! If I were you I would stand back, I'm not altogether happy with the way he is looking at you. May I suggest that you try the Aquarian husband?

Now who will make me another offer? Yes, Madam, I hear you, but, to be honest, you look a trifle domesticated. I expect you would like a man who would appreciate your home-making talents ... yes? No doubt he would be more welcome if he could knock you up some fitted cupboards or shelves whenever a creative mood descended. Right? And you would be happy to give up your career and devote yourself to him? Do watch out, Madam, he is getting a nasty curl to his lower lip. Why not shop around? You would only be disappointed with this particular model. Not your kind at all.

Did I hear a husky voice enquiring as to the nature of his type? Well, let's see. She could be rather like your good self. He likes glamour and femininity. He won't mind if you have a career provided it doesn't threaten him in any way; he must be top dog. You will need to be an excellent hostess. Don't worry about your cooking, he will arrange the catering, but you had better be the mistress of small-talk. If on top of all this you are affectionate, highly-sexed and fashionable, then he's yours. No ... please refrain from leading him by the hand. Allow him to take you ... now you've got it right — and also probably got it made! With the right lady, Leo is Mr Perfection. Generous, loyal and dependable, but with the wrong woman he can become overbearing and a bully. Therefore, at all times he should be discriminating and cautious; many a Lion has been swept into marriage while still in the euphoric state of newly-discovered love, only to be later disillusioned and deflated. The young cub needs longer than most to explore and parley in the jungle before choosing a mate. It takes time for him to mature to the point where he can accept his own shortcomings, but when he eventually succeeds in doing so he will be better fitted to tie that important knot.

LEO WIFE

To any man looking for the proverbial "little woman" to fill that empty gap in his life, one who will stay at home, look after the kids and be satisfied with a monthly outing to the cinema, followed by the monthly love session, then my advice is — run, before this lady gets to hear about it, and tears you to pieces with her well-manicured fingernails. And you, sir, with the long hair and denims, I suspect that you are wasting your time: the Leo wife is not for the man who is forever chasing new causes or revolutions to the exclusion of everything else. Any more than she would be a good proposition for the dedicated doctor, scientist, policeman etc. Surely you are not expecting her to sit at home night after night while you are out answering the needs of humanity? If so, then you will land in a divorce court before you know what has hit you. No, gentlemen, this is a special lady, and she requires a special man — sophisticated, intelligent, elegant and loyal. Naturally he needs also to be crazy about her, lead a busy social life and, above all else, be prepared to be taken over. A little demanding, you may conclude. But consider: she does, after all have plenty to offer. You will be proud to be seen with her, she can communicate with everyone, from the most humble to the most eminent. She will do anything for those she loves without considering repayment, materially or emotionally. But what about her homemaking? She is a great hostess. Her cooking? Your door will always be open to friends. Needlework? Oh, for heaven's sake! This is a *Leo* lady we are talking about. She can learn, if she deigns to, but if that is all you are worried about then I emphatically insist that you leave this section. There are plenty of men who are attracted to our Leo woman, although chances are she will not be acquainted with her own needs until fairly late in life. The only problem is that she may stumble and fall emotionally several times before she reaches that happy state of maturity.

LEO AND DIVORCE

Divorce for the Lion is failure, and so it is taken badly. If you have found marriage difficult, then divorce will be equally so. You tend to go through three stages: 1: The "I don't want to live" phase. Quickly followed by ... 2: The "I don't want to discuss it. Do as you please" phase. 3: The "I never needed you anyway" phase. Ideally, stage 3 should be reached as soon as possible. The first is too destructive and hurtful for all concerned and stage 2 can be bloody expensive. Before you know what has happened you will have given all your mutual possessions away. Too many memories, you'll rationalize. You will have committed yourself to ridiculous alimony, because you can't do anything on a small scale. Besides, it is undignified to quarrel about money, or so you believe. However, you may change your mind when you find you are left without a roof over your head! Yes, stage 3 is the only way to go, and once you have arrived you will return to living again. Your temperament is such that you need admirers, the more the merrier, to give you back your confidence and waistline. A Lion without confidence is a sorry sight, but at least one good thing will arise from the mess: that is, self-knowledge.

As previously mentioned, it is difficult for you to be objective about yourself, although I doubt that your estranged mate is so hampered. But should this life become unbearable, due to the insults aimed at your head, then you must be philosophical. Remember, he, or she, once found you irresistible. Clearly then, you cannot be as monstrous, nor as vile, as they now say. Any reserves of logic you can draw upon will be invaluable at this point. For example: "You are a selfish, egotistical bully," should be translated as: "You are a proud and strong person, but one who tends to overlook the feelings of others on occasions."

Example 2: "You are an irresponsible bitch who cannot resist anything in trousers." This should be taken as: "You are sometimes too generous to strangers." Example 3: "You are a conceited, vain, good-time crazy waster." Roughly translated this becomes: "You are a person who takes a pride in their appearance, one who likes people and their constant company."

By now you should be getting the idea. If not ... I give up! Remember, the quicker your bruised ego heals, the quicker you will be able to recover and concentrate on the business of living. You know that the rest of the world misses the sun when it hides behind a cloud, so do hurry and come and join us sometimes.

LEO EX-HUSBAND

Once you have recovered from the rigours of divorce you can usually be considered a realistic candidate for ex-husband of the year. It's true that as a hubby you may have failed, but you are darned hard to overtake in this particular race. Your generosity does not die with the demise of love; if anything it increases and could be a little embarrassing for husband or wife number 2. They are never going to be able to live up to you, and I sincerely hope they refrain from trying. Neither are you the possessive type who hangs around the ex-wife hoping for a crumb of affection. You have far too much self-respect for that. Either you are invited or you don't go at all. Placed in such a position, you acquire all the wisdom of Solomon and allow your ex to be the guide. If she wants to see you or requires your help, then she can rely on you. If she prefers you out of her life, you may be hurt but you comply. You are even prepared to return to the matrimonial bed for a night or two, provided you have received a gilt-edged invitation, but you will not consider reconciliation. Once you have departed you will not return. Divorce meant that you had to admit to one failure. To return, then, would mean admitting that this too was a mistake. I'm afraid that this isn't feasible for you. Eventually you may both drift into becoming good friends and there may even be occasions when you will forget that you were ever married at all. In future, you will be proud of anything she achieves professionally and will probably be best man when she re-marries. Mind you, what her second husband is going to say about that I shudder to think, but you must try not to be too hurt if he suggests that you make your visits less frequent. Be flattered he is obviously growing sick and tired of being compared to such a paragon of virtue. You may be tempted to indulge in some revenge at this stage and deliberately stick around; but you are supposed to be kind, generous and magnanimous, are you not? So now is the time to prove it. Return to your lair and shower some extra attention on that new Lioness, chances are she is beginning to feel a little left out.

LEO EX-WIFE

You are not the ideal ex, but there are certainly a few worse than you. Like your male counterpart you drift through three phases, finally reaching the point where you allow your first husband to be your guide when it comes to your future relationship. But if the poor man left you, then you are going to be suffering from hurt pride and this may lead to some unreasonable financial demands, as you try to make him pay. But come off it, you know as well as I do that it wasn't all his fault; even if it were and you are suffering from a never-to-be-mended heart, no amount of money will ever heal it, not until it's ready. All you will achieve and acquire is his alienation and hostility. Eventually he will not be able to remember anything pleasant about you at all. At least remember that if you insist on keeping a check on his finances, the procedure could become somewhat demeaning. Are you prepared to soil yourself in this fashion? I doubt it. Leave it up to your solicitor, be reasonable and life will be less fraught. You will be able to forget the past a good deal quicker this way and get on with the present and the future. You probably have a trail of admirers just waiting their chance. Try to preserve that ego of yours; you know how important it is for you to remain confident. Do not allow that ex of yours to undermine you in any way. If he wants to insult you, put a realistic interpretation on his words. Example 1: "You spend too much time in front of the mirror and not enough in the kitchen." This translated could mean: "You are not prepared to become a drudge and you value

your appearance." Example 2: "You are a selfish, oversexed bitch."
Surely he means: "You are an ambitious, passionate lady!" And after
you'd just met, didn't he say as much? Yes, there is no doubt about it,
when you are going through a divorce, it's self-preservation that
counts. And you have plenty of that. So let's have a quick, clean fight
with no fouls. You have more important things to do, haven't you? I
thought so!

LEO AND THE COMMUNE

To put it briefly, this arrangement can only be considered if the other
members of the community are ready for a dictator. Otherwise forget
it. No way are you going to muck in babysitting for others, neither are
you about to do their dirty work. Yes, you'll take command and
organize everyone; in fact, in this capacity, you are difficult to beat.
But how long you would stick to this lifestyle is debatable. Three
months? Three weeks? Three hours? You like your privacy, to be able
to close your door and forget the outside world. And you certainly
prefer to decide who will enter your lair. The constant popping in and
out by other people can be guaranteed to drive you around the bend
and far away. As a serious mode of existence for you, the commune
will leave a lot to be desired.

LEO AND COHABITATION

Provided there is an emotional involvement, this can be a satisfactory
way of life for the Leo. He is not as insecure as the Cancerian nor as
conventional as the Taurean. The Lion simply wants to be with the
adored one, but he isn't the easiest person in the world to live with, so
the relationship may not last for very long. However, as long as you
are honest about your intentions and do not lead your mate to believe
that your affair will develop into marriage, then all will be well. A little
piece of legal paper means nothing to the mature Lion. You make
your own rules, and your strong love and ability to care for another
person should, you believe, be all that is required to make a happy life
for both of you. And if the relationship does manage to survive the
day-to-day problems then it will end in marriage, but you won't be
expecting it. So be warned, you more insecure members of the human
race.

LEO LOVER — MALE

When a Lion sets up house with a new Lioness he doesn't want to
come home to pretty florals, furniture with spindly legs that look as if
they will collapse under the weight of an eight-year-old; neither is he
attracted to highly-polished tables that require hourly dusting.
However, do not run away with the idea that he is a slob. Far from it,
he wants to be greeted by an elegant lady, subtle lighting and big, soft
chairs that he can truly relax in while he sips a well-earned whisky
from a crystal glass. And in spite of the evening arrangements — and
there will be plenty — he will not budge from his relaxation for a good

hour, at which time he will slowly rise, bathe and change. She, meantime, sits in readiness, ticking with impatience. But there is nothing to be gained from nagging. He does things at his own pace. Besides, the clock is probably set at the Leo time, so she is helpless. He may be a big, cuddly softy, but question his authority or threaten him as head of the household, and you should prepare to do battle. These are some of the problems connected with sharing the Lion's den; but do not despair, he has his compensations. If he is truly attached to the female in question, he will not run around chasing everything in skirts, furthermore he will be happy to — nay, will insist on taking over the financial responsibilities. Finally, he will not want this lady to be a drudge. Any outside help will be provided if humanly possible. On the nights spent at home he will be more than willing to join in with culinary experiments. If the relationship works well, marriage will be the end result, but it is best not to rely on it. Living a day at a time is the wisest way when you take on a Leo lover.

LEO LOVER — FEMALE

The female Leo is very similar in habit to the male as a lover. This is a confident woman and not one who wants, or necessarily expects, marriage. The maternal instinct either surfaces late in life or not at all. Certainly the thought of being surrounded by two or three children does little for her except to produce feelings of horror or the eruption of a rash. In love she is passionate and sincere, charging in ready to give all and, provided she is mature, cohabitation could turn out to be a satisfactory arrangement. But it is essential that she be honest with herself: if she is secretly hoping for wedding bells with a lover who is vehemently anti-matrimony she will probably be disappointed in believing that cohabitation will lead to a change of heart. If they are in love, however, and want to be together, content to live in the present, then all will be fine.

Of course, this situation may lead to marriage, but she would be unwise to rely on it. The Leo lady has a lot to give, but not in the kitchen or around the house. She will make her man proud of her in other ways. He will never be able to compare her to an unmade bed, she will always be ready with encouragement, affection and sex. So her man may have to rustle up dinner occasionally, or run the vacuum over the carpet, but surely he will decide that she is worth it.

LEO CHILD AND DIVORCE

With children of this sign there is one thing of which you can be sure. No matter how helpless they may appear on the surface, underneath they are in fact well in control of themselves and the situation at hand. This doesn't mean they aren't upset; on the contrary, they could be quite shattered for a while. If it is a boy we are discussing he will decide that Mum needs him and that he must now become the man of the house. Conversely, if he is left with Dad, then he will believe that he must be responsible and help to pull this grown-man through a difficult phase. These feelings, on either count, should be encouraged. There is nothing like thought for others to take your mind off yourself. However, a word of advice, no matter how badly your spouse may have behaved never, but never, attempt to blacken their character in the little chap's eyes. He will lose respect for you and jump to the missing parent's defence. Keep explanations on the departure simple, avoiding lurid details. He can't cope with ugliness or petty behaviour. Remember, everything that is said about the missing parent in his presence will be understood. Don't underestimate him for a minute. He will listen in on telephone conversations you have with mother or friend, if he thinks he may learn more, but nothing the erring spouse of yours has done will dim his devotion. Not yet, anyway. If Dad is a louse, or Mum a true bitch, then he will discover this fact for himself in his own good time. And, what's more important, when he is able to cope with it. The Lion is a bad judge of character, so do not be too surprised if, even when the facts are placed before him, he still prefers to ignore them. In the meantime, as he grows, he will try to take over the dominant role in the house. A female cub will become "Little Mother Earth" and the male cub will be forever trying to think of ways to earn some extra cash in an effort to contribute to the running costs of the house. Accept all of this, for young Lions also need to feel important, and in a one-parent home they have the chance to positively shine, and it shouldn't be denied them. Discipline should be firm but, gentle. Hysterics make them stubborn and laxity will make them unbelievably arrogant and bumptious. Logic and love with special understanding are all that are required to keep this child on the direct road to mature adulthood.

LEO CHILD AND REMARRIAGE

With a reasonable child, all you need to do is to beg permission. Yes ... I'm afraid it may be just a little like that. The cub has probably become so used to taking the responsible role in your life that it may not be relinquished just like that. But the prospective parent should be gradually allowed to enter this child's life, visits slowly increasing. Don't throw him or her in the deep end; chances are that they will not swim. Let them observe for themselves the things that love can give Mum or Dad that they cannot, but always include them in your laughter and outings where possible. The biggest danger is that sensitive ego, which can result in feelings of not being wanted any more, therefore Leo children must not only be made to accept and recognize what the new parent can contribute, but must also be aware of the place they are supposed to fill in the general scheme of things. Furthermore, let them know just how important they are to the family unit. They must not be undermined any more than is absolutely necessary. For example, if the child has been used to carrying the shopping for Mum, there is no reason why this should not carry on. The only difference is that now you go to the shops in the new parent's car and it is only necessary to carry the shopping to the car park. Get the idea? Both are helping the adored parent. Acceptance comes slowly, and impatience, resentment or irritation will be sensed. This is a sensitive child despite the arrogance. Keep young Leo's ego and heart intact and you will not find him impossible. Difficult, perhaps. But then, aren't we all?

CONCLUSION

The relationship you decide upon in life is, of course, up to you. Chances are that you will experiment a good deal before settling for the lifestyle you believe to be best suited to you. Even a commune may appeal for a while, although you would need absolute power for it to attract you in the smallest degree.

Bachelorhood is a stage we all experience in life and you, as a Lion, will enjoy discovering sex and the opposite sex for several years before you are ready to consider living with one mate. After all, why should you when you can have ten? The single status is sure to seem lonely eventually and you will grow disenchanted with it; at this point marriage may be sought. Your biggest problem is that you are usually temporarily ruled by emotion and are a dead loss when it comes to judging character. Multiple marriages are frequently associated with this sign as a result, for some Lions never look at others objectively.

So what is left? Cohabitation? Yes, this can be satisfactory. You have the ability to give and the confidence to overcome any niggling insecurities. All you require is a mate who is likewise inclined, then you could be all set for great happiness. If it eventually leads to marriage ... great. If not, you can always be philosophical, can't you?

LEO MARRIAGE CHANCES QUIZ

Answer these questions honestly and score 3 for yes, 2 for sometimes or unsure, and 1 for no.

1. Do you have a busy social life?
2. Do you care what others think of you?
3. Do you want others to be impressed by your choice of mate?
4. Do you have expensive tastes?
5. Do you have a sensitive ego?
6. Are you a regular party-giver?
7. Do you prefer the opposite sex to your own?
8. Do you think others are at all envious of you?
9. Is success important to you?
10. Are you influenced by flattery? (Ask your mate.)
11. Do you insist on respect from others?
12. Is divorce a necessary evil in your terms?
13. Are you generous?
14. Do you let go easily when a relationship ends?

15. Would you be indignant if told your sexual technique was lacking in some way?
16. Do you accompany your mate when he/she buys a new item of clothing? (Tights and underpants don't count!)
17. Are you sensitive to your surroundings?
18. Do you need a mate who makes you feel good?
19. Are you sensitive to criticism?
20. Do you believe in boarding schools for children?

ANSWERS

1 — 30: You are not a typical Leo. Chances are that you have several planets in Capricorn or Virgo. Therefore, your chances of matrimonial happiness are improved. Read both the sections devoted to these signs and you will find a good deal of yourself in them. If you are already divorced, it is unlikely to happen again, for ninety per cent of the time you choose your mate wisely.

31 — 50: This is the score of the typical Leo, but you are lucky and have more of the virtues of this sign than the vices. You are a delight to know. Whilst you are sure to have married unwisely once, probably when very young, in mature life your chances of finding happiness are greatly increased, although the relationship concerned may stop short of that legal piece of paper.

51 — 60: You are a typical Leo but, regrettably, possess more of the vices than the virtues of your sign. You care too much about the opinions of others and rely heavily on them for approval. Because of this, you choose a mate solely on their ability to impress. Not a good idea. If you fail to recognize this fault, you may continue to enter and depart from the marriage stakes yearly.

VIRGO
(the Virgin)
August 24 — September 23

Planet: Mercury
Colour: Grey or navy blue
Partners: (In general) Capricorn and Taurus
Countries: Greece, Crete, Virginia, Brazil, Turkey, West Indies
Cities: Paris, Lyons, Heidelberg, Jerusalem, Athens, Boston
Famous Virgoans: Lyndon B. Johnson, Henry Ford II, Sophia Loren, Anne Bancroft, Leonard Bernstein, Greta Garbo, Arnold Palmer

GENERAL CHARACTERISTICS

You are a practical, diligent and down-to-earth worker with a competent, discriminating intellect. You gather knowledge from every conceivable source and have the ability to memorize and retain what you have learned. You are scientific, perceptive and very alert. You do not stop learning when you graduate from school, but keep it up throughout the rest of your life.

Virgo rules the bowels and, just as they assimilate the food, so the mind of the Virgoan assimilates food for thought. This process makes you very critical and discriminating. You analyse everything and, to others less like yourself, may seem to be constantly finding fault. In reality this is the way your mind works and no harm is intended. You simply have to categorize everything and see it for what it is in comparison with everything else. You are clever at speech and writing but, unless there are other influences on your personal birth chart, you may seem monotonous and dry. Mercury's influence makes you understand human intellectual emotions but you rarely experience the gamut of human passions yourself. However, you can be quite tactful because of your practicality and the way that you analyse and observe. Generally, though, you haven't much sympathy for others.

You are usually modest and unassuming, content to live in the background; not requiring constant company, you often want to be left alone and are so cool and evenly balanced that you almost never lose your temper. You are content to work quietly and unpretentiously at your chosen job, yet are very proud of your mental powers, whether they happen to be extraordinary or not. Because you are so shy and retiring you often fail to inspire the confidence of others in the same way as an extrovert type. You may seem to be less reserved to those that know you, but your inner reserve never melts. However, you may be considered very interesting to the people who would be afraid of the aggressive Aries or Leo. Your innate humility and willingness to serve humanity may endear you to the gentler folk.

You lack inspiration but are very good and methodical in your routine work, liking detail, but you need to be careful not to become so obsessed by it that you don't see the forest for the trees. You are usually very clever at mathematics and might do well as a statistician or, if you show more inspiration, a businessman or an economist. You would, however, prefer business to the professions and might show an aptitude for law and medicine. You are very quick to see and take advantage of opportunities in commercial concerns. When it comes to money you are thrifty and saving. While you may not have the talents of a financier, your bank book is always balanced accurately.

You are somewhat self-centred when it comes to love and do not like the idea of either conquest or self-sacrifice. However, you make a reliable spouse and the kind of parent who does not spoil a child, rather giving the understanding and security that aids development. You have an instinctive sense of balance in diet and are also very sensible in taking care of your own health and that of other people.

VIRGO AND MARRIAGE

Female Virgoans are not particularly romantic, but you are methodical and well organized. You are, no doubt, a gem in the business office, and when it comes to managing a home nobody will be more efficient and practical. Everything will run like clockwork; but you tend to calculate the fun out of everyday life. Although you may take care of material detail with precision, the human emotion and happiness that go into real home-making are outside your ken. You are not the type to create jealousy in members of your own sex, for you are cool and intellectual rather than warm and emotional with men. You calculate every move.

The male Virgoan tends to attract the type of woman just described, and the attraction will not be particularly romantic. But at least you are very helpful in a practical way. When it comes to handling a crisis you are just the guy to call for. Your affections are usually diverted into intellectual channels; you may be somewhat cerebral in your intimate relations. Some Virgoans can be cold and materialistic in love. Others will dedicate themselves to a worthy cause that enlists their minds more than their emotions.

You will often be accused of being aloof and solitary because you like to keep people at a distance, so you have more acquaintances than close friends. You prefer to divide your affections among a lot of people. But although considerate, you are never wholeheartedly in love.

You are critical of those who cffer you their affections; you tend to analyse them so thoroughly that you cannot help but find fault. When you do love, you don't sweep others off their feet by ardour and depth of emotion, but you can make your loved ones very comfortable indeed. When you fail to find a personal love you may be a blessing to humanity instead. Many doctors and nurses are born under this sign and they serve their patients conscientiously and with great consideration. Because of your ability quickly to sense the faults of others, it is not surprising that this is all too often' the sign of the confirmed bachelor or spinster, a fact you sometimes regret later in life. You are undoubtedly intellectual and quick-witted but, for all that, you can be rather stupid in human relations. When your lover is distraught and behaving in a confused fashion, there is no point in reaching for the nearest book on psychology; all that is needed is a shoulder to sob on and a little bit of affection. Why you always manage to overlook the simplicity of such a situation is difficult to say. If you consciously try to feel more and think less, your relationship could be a great deal happier, but then you wouldn't be a typical Virgoan, would you?

Petty fault-finding is another danger to marriage, and with your intelligence you must realize when you are being unreasonable. Why not try to bite back those carping and sarcastic words? So what if she didn't iron your newspaper and your boot laces this morning? If you go to work with an untidy *Times* and crumpled laces, it really isn't the end of the world. Of course, the easiest thing to do is to make certain that you don't get yourself hitched to a highly sensitive and emotional personality. Try to find someone with a similar outlook to life as your own. Marriage can work extremely well for the Virgoan, you have an ability to work hard on others' behalf, but, please, a little more feeling, a little more romance. You will be surprised at the difference this makes.

VIRGO HUSBAND

If you have ever been involved with a Virgoan man then you know he is not the easiest character in the world to please. In fact, many a

Virgoan-experienced lady will insist that anyone who seriously believes him to be their mate is heading for disaster. In many cases this would be true, as in the following instances:

Enemy No. 1: The ultra-feminine, hyper-sensitive woman. You know the type — the one who is reduced to tears by even the slightest criticism. She is far too demanding on an emotional level for our Virgoan friend, and if she is foolish enough to imagine that he will rush home from work and passionately sweep her into his arms, she is in for a big let-down. The truth is that when he does arrive home, probably late, the first thing he will do is pass a remark about the dirt on the new carpet. And, as he reaches over to place that timid peck on her expectant cheek, his eyes will be riveted on a half-filled ashtray behind her. In the first bloom of love he may sigh and rush around tight-lipped for half an hour, clearing up those offending items. But at some point he will begin to give utterance to his complaints. Eventually she may either go back to Mother or have a nervous breakdown. Chances are he won't even notice her absence, he will be far too busy cleaning up the mess the ambulance men left in their wake.

Enemy No. 2: The narcissist or the egotist. Any woman who expects this man to spend his time flattering, cajoling or coaxing is in for a shock. If he notices the original model dress that she is wearing, it will be because the label has been inadvertently left on, or there is a flaw in it somewhere that others have overlooked. "How do I look, darling?" is a question one should never ask a Virgoan, expecting a compliment; it is more than likely she will receive a slap in the face. "Is that lipstick or nail varnish supposed to match? If so I'm afraid they aren't quite right. However, you look O.K." Eventually she will become too afraid to ask and will begin to search for ego-building somewhere else.

But enough of these negatives. He does have his good points, points which are clearly enhanced by the right lady. And the ideal woman will be the closest thing to a paragon of virtue you have ever met. It is important that she be intellectually active, almost certainly a woman with a career, for this will enable them to exchange views in the evening, providing him with a source of intellectual stimulation. He will be genuinely interested in what she is trying to achieve, and the money contributed will be welcomed by such a practical character; in his book, anything that helps to fight the cost of living is to be applauded. He will even volunteer to help in the house, if not on a fifty/fifty basis, then at least on a forty/sixty. And when she is sick he will be the epitome of efficiency, organizing the domestic chores so well that she could begin to suffer from feelings of being dispensable. Yes, the Virgoan husband has plenty going for him on the credit side. He will work miracles with the finances; wasteful and extravagant behaviour will not be tolerated. He will also be scrupulously faithful.

He truly cannot be bothered with sordid little affairs. He believes there is no point in being married if that is the way you want to carry on.

The Virgoan also makes an efficient parent, although the family will need to be small and the timing right. If there are financial problems, then another mouth to feed would send him screaming out of the front door, although later he will no doubt return in order to sit down and work out how they are going to manage.

The wrong lady may well describe him as cold, mechanical and clinical, but to the right one he is Mr Dependable himself, and a devoted lover, husband and father.

VIRGO WIFE

Do you like your woman to be smouldering with passion, desire and unspoken longings — Cleopatra and Helen of Troy all rolled into one? Do you yearn for someone who will worship the ground you walk upon and melt like butter in your arms? If you do, then I am afraid you are in the wrong section. Why not try the Scorpio or Leo lady? The Virgoan wife will only worship the ground you walk on if she owns it. Yes, she is definitely the "please don't forget to take your shoes off before walking across the new carpet" type. As for melting in your arms, she will be more adept at making you melt with one of her icy stares when your glass leaves a ring on her highly polished table. This is a woman who loves with her mind and needs someone likewise inclined, a man she can discuss, debate and do battle with.

It is also essential that her husband be honest with her in everything from finance to other women. Yet, strangely enough, it would be most out of character for her to desert him over some insignificant affair — provided that he has confessed all, of course. Do not insult her intelligence with a tissue of lies, she'll know ... you can depend on it!

She is graciously aware of the fact that we all have our faults, but her man must possess the kind that she can accept. It's perfectly all right for him to be a hypochondriac, for instance, as long as he puts his clothes away before crawling into bed. And she won't throw hysterics if he arrives back late from work, provided he is capable when he does come home. But despite her observance of a strict code of behaviour, there is no one more capable at running a house, a job and two children. In this respect she is a miracle-worker. Furthermore she is always careful with her appearance, invariably appearing neat, clean and tidy. A trifle aloof? Possibly, but there are plenty of men who find that a woman who wants to revolve her life around the bedroom is a bit of a drag! And it simply would not be practical to expect all women to be sex bombs, now would it?

VIRGO AND DIVORCE

Now let us assume that you have married your Virgoan and it simply didn't work, and yet you cannot leave because you believe that it would break their heart. Rubbish! If you really believe that you must both go your separate ways then all you have to do is say so. Your Virgoan will probably help you to pack; don't expect to have a grovelling character begging you not to leave. However, this doesn't necessarily mean that it will be easy for you to dump this individual.

The material aspect to divorce is the one which will create most of your problems. If your Virgoan is a woman then she will extract the maximum out of her wayward spouse. You may strike lucky; she may be reasonable if you refrain from attempting to duck your responsibilities; but if you imagine that you are going to get away scot free, then you are in for a tough time. Never lose sight of the fact that this is the sign of the nagger. Eventually she'll talk you into submission. Anything, you'll say, anything, only leave me alone! But what if the deserted spouse is male? Then the opposite, of course, applies. He will do his darnedest to avoid putting his hand in his pocket, and life could become very unpleasant.

It is true to say, then, that divorce does not bring out the best in the Virgoan. And it is not an experience members of this sign will ever wish to repeat. When the situation is unavoidable, however, the best way to go is for you to throw yourself into your career or job for a while. Attempt to keep that critical and active head busy. If you, as a Virgoan, can fill your days with constant activity, then you will sleep well at night, thus keeping thoughts of retribution at bay. Eventually you'll need more out of life, and then go ahead and treat yourself to a new wardrobe, accept invitations, and try to avoid spending time dissecting your prospective date. You are always going to be able to find something wrong. Let's be honest: at this stage in life the object of the operation is not to find another life-mate but to get you back into the swing of living again. Lastly, any queries or complaints that you have about the divorce should be handled by your solicitor. You may feel perfectly able to deal with that erring spouse, but all you will do is make them bloody-minded and this will hold up legal procedure for an unnecessary period of time. And do try to look on the bright side. At least divorce will have taught you one thing — that is that even you are not perfect and can, if only occasionally, make mistakes. Perhaps in future you will be kinder in your judgement of others.

VIRGO EX-HUSBAND

The ex-husband isn't exactly a role in which you Virgoans excel. Your biggest fault is a tendency towards continued bickering over possessions and money. If you acknowledge this fact and try to be reasonable, then maybe life will not be too bad. Otherwise it's going to be sheer hell. "I want the silver spoons! They came from *my* Aunt Maude as a wedding present." When greeted with this your ex-spouse, if she has any sense at all, will throw them at you and if she chooses to be just as petty it will take a lifetime for you both to decide just who has what. Why not tell yourself that peace of mind is worth more than a set of spoons, or even two sets of spoons?

Now let us assume that this phase is well behind you. What kind of ex-husband will you make? Still not the perfect one, I'm afraid. You are a worrier. "Is she all right?" you ask yourself. "Looked a bit pale in court." Before you know what has happened you are on the way to her house (or yours, if you haven't been canny), you knock. She stands before you in a seductive negligee. What *is* she doing dressed like that at three in the afternoon? The answer becomes apparent for behind her, equally informally dressed, is a refugee from a pop concert. Strange how this kind of situation is always so hilarious in films but so embarrassing in life. You cough, splutter and mumble a few words, before departing at top speed. You arrive back home ... then it starts. "How dare she put you in such a position?" Of course, you've completely forgotten that you hadn't received an invitation to visit. "And how could she get involved with that kid?" Again it has slipped your mind that you are now DIVORCED. "Doesn't she care what the neighbours think?" Consider ... they aren't your neighbours any more, are they? So what are you getting so steamed up about? You may as well face it, it will be some time before you realize that she is no longer part of your life. But do try to wake up soon, otherwise you may never get around to sorting out your own problems. Worry about your own life, job, sexual affairs. Where is that cool intellect? Now is as good a time as any to bring it into play. If that ex of yours needs you, she'll yell — good and loud! Until then, keep out. Think about it.

VIRGO EX-WIFE

Hardly your forte, this ex-wife business. Never mind, it takes a while to get used to it — that big, empty, lonely bed, and the fact that you can have dinner at twelve if you so desire. And what about the housework? Now the slob has finally gone there is precious little to do. And you are still half expecting to hear his key in the door, aren't you? It is these small everyday occurrences that take a bit of adapting to. And how is the divorce going? Taking longer than you had anticipated? What's the matter, isn't he prepared to hand over his wages? The time has arrived for you to adopt a different philosophy. There is no reason at all why he shouldn't meet his obligations, you protest. But think ... do you earn as much as he? Is he out of work? Don't know? Well, I suggest that you check up. Were you both too busy to get around to starting a family? If you can answer yes to any of these then I am sorry, but you cannot expect him to pay through the nose simply because he had the pleasure of being married to you once. If you are left with the children and precious little income then it becomes a different story, otherwise surely peace of mind is better than unpleasantness? Unpleasantness that can be caused over a pittance.

Of course, if you are going to become self-righteous or "principled" then there is nothing anyone can say except, start looking to the future as quickly as possible. Tie a neat blue bow on your broken marriage and forget it. You may not be the greatest socializer in the world, but surely you must receive some invitations, and unless you accept the occasional one your friends will stop asking. A good book may be better than bad company, but you never know who you might meet unless you actually go out. Why not change your image? A new hairstyle, for instance, could do wonders for your ego, a couple of new dresses, maybe in a style a little more daring than is your usual. And on the practical level, if you are still occupying the matrimonial home, why not decorate it? Start with the bedroom ... Any or all of these things will make the world of difference to you.

I'm sure you don't want to become a nagging, impotent shrew, do you? Make that ex of yours regret the day he ever had the temerity to leave. I'm not suggesting that you take him back; the object of this exercise is ego-building. There is no point in convincing yourself that you are past caring, or that you have finished with men. (Haven't we all, dear, until the next time!) Cool, even cold, you may be, but you are still human, whether you like it or not.

VIRGO AND COHABITATION

Provided you have been made to feel that this is a practical idea, maybe you will consider setting up home with your lover. But there is no point in your loved one declaring, "I love you and I must be with you." You will simply doubt their sanity, and your common sense, for ever getting involved with such a ridiculous creature in the first place. But if either of you are waiting for a divorce, this is a practical enough reason for you to live together. Conversely, if it can be proven that two can live as cheaply as one, then this too is a constructive reason for cohabitation. But generally speaking, you as a Virgoan will decide that you may just as well be married. Your lover will be wasting his or her time to dare to suggest that you may get to know each other better before taking that plunge, though this argument may work with you if you have been married before, for in this instance you will not be quite so sure of your infallible judgement.

However, assuming that you have agreed to set up home there is no reason at all why this arrangement should not work quite well. You must consciously try to control that sharp tongue, because you will realize that your lover can pick up and leave whenever the mood takes them. But, eventually, such self-restraint could become harder to maintain. I certainly wouldn't like to be around the day it finally gives out. You will positively burst forth with six months of stifled complaint. All, no doubt, itemized and labelled.

There is no getting away from it, you find it difficult to be yourself in such circumstances. So cohabitation isn't the ideal solution for you.

VIRGO LOVER — MALE

In this instance the above title is at fault, for this character is hardly the most serious contender for Romeo of the year, as his lady will soon discover. Please don't get me wrong, this doesn't mean he isn't crazy about her, but the fact is he will never show it in poetry or song. Neither will he sweep her into his arms on the hour throughout the day. No, if that is what you are looking for then you are reading the wrong section. But if you are looking for a man who stays calm in a crisis, can reduce any problem by sensible discussion, and who will worry and care about your physical well-being, then here he is. If you are a career lady, he is happy to help around the house, just as long as it is not too dirty in the first place. If it is, needless to say it will be your dirt and not his.

This individual may not be over demanding emotionally or sexually, but practically, that is a different matter. You will be blissfully happy with him, provided you clean the bathroom after you, put your clothes away and refrain from leaving tights and knickers about or taps dripping. If you manage this, your Virgoan will see no reason at all why you shouldn't be married. Of course, if you want to remain single, then you had better make a fast exit.

VIRGO LOVER — FEMALE

If you like the simple, simpering, dimpled type of lady — hard luck, for you won't find her here. Miss Virgo is slim, attractive, neat and detached. Many men find her a bit of a challenge, but if you imagine that under the cold exterior there beats a violently passionate heart, you are about to be disillusioned. In fact, under that cool exterior lies a cool interior. Fortunately for her there are plenty of admirers who believe that there is more to a woman than sheer sexuality. To the ambitious type, fighting up that slippery ladder of success, she will be invaluable. It isn't a prerequisite that you become Mr Big, but she will always find a positive solution to your negative mood. "So all right, Mr Simpkins was promoted over your head, but then he was more experienced, keep at it dear, and your turn will come!" Or maybe your boss turned down your new proposals. So they were ahead of their time, she'll reason, give the old man time to catch up with you.

Yes, the Virgoan lady will berate her lover for leaving dirty socks under the bed, but when it comes to the important things, relax; she is on your side. You will be astounded by her energy. Not only will your nest shine like a new pin, but she will manage it on top of her job and one hundred other things. However, like her male counterpart, provided you haven't grown to detest each other in six months then the practical side of her will expect marriage. Living in sin doesn't feel particularly sinful to her.

VIRGO AND THE COMMUNE

At some point, the communal lifestyle could appeal to the Virgoan, but whether the other members of the establishment are ready for this character is another matter. They will be expected to live up to certain standards of cleanliness and tidiness. This is a hard worker who will energetically put heart and soul into the general good of the group. It isn't necessary for the Virgoan to have a partner, in fact, he or she will probably work more efficiently without one. Remember that dedicated doctor? Well, here you will have a shining example of what this sign is prepared to do, and sacrifice, on behalf of other people. Nevertheless, the Virgoan is human and could eventually need more intimacy, at which point he or she will be off. Whilst the remaining members of the commune may initially heave a sigh of relief, of one thing you can be sure: it won't be long before the Virgoan is greatly missed.

VIRGO CHILD AND DIVORCE

This is a situation where the Virgoan's intellect and cool can prove invaluable, provided, that is, the reasons for the break-up are explained. The absence of a parent will naturally incite curiosity and this must be satisfied. "Mummy and Daddy can no longer get on ... ": the Virgo child is perfectly able to understand this from personal experience of falling out with playmates. People are so difficult sometimes. No wonder Mummy couldn't cope with Daddy! One of the "no-nos" in this case is an emotional outburst. This makes the young Virgoan feel uneasy, not knowing how to react and therefore being confused and feeling inadequate. Neither will you achieve anything by drawing attention to the missing parent's faults; the child is probably more aware of them than you and certainly won't need reminding. Keep that active little head occupied with new interests to prevent it indulging in self-pity. This does not mean that sweetness and light will reign for the erring spouse. Initially there will be the big freeze but, if you are both patient, your offspring will eventually come round. Divorce is never a happy experience for any child but the Virgoan is better equipped to cope than most.

VIRGO CHILD AND REMARRIAGE

Just as your Virgoans take divorce in their stride, so the remarriage should be no problem — unless it becomes a regular occurrence, of course! Here again the approach must be intellectual. A parent who descends with tears in eyes, throws arms around the child's neck, wailing, "Darling, I've found you a new Daddy!" is asking for trouble. This youngster will screw up its nose, struggle out of the imprisoning embrace and mutter: "Big deal." That just isn't the way to go. You would elicit a more favourable reaction if you informed the child that you are taking on Mr Brown because he is willing to pay you each night for sleeping with him! Young Virgo could at least appreciate the practicalities of this! No ... simply say that you have met someone you want to marry (be positive), because you both like the same things and he or she makes you happy. Leave the lovey-dovey stuff out of it; you'd only embarrass the little puritan. Once the ice is broken, throw your new love and your child in at the deep end. You'll be surprised how quickly they both learn to swim. The Virgoan's adaptability is well developed. This child will soon adjust to a new life and a new parent, if treated like an adult and not a baby.

CONCLUSION

Now is the right time to take a second look at the Virgoan in conjunction with various relationships, in an effort to help you decide which is the right road in life for you.

The commune? This is ideal for the lonely Virgoan whose life has no purpose, but whether it is a lifelong proposition is debatable. Only you can answer that.

Bachelorhood is a common state of affairs with members of this sign, and one that sometimes lasts for life. It is never easy for you to find that soul mate and many Virgoans will just not settle for second best. However, just because there is no alternative doesn't make it any more preferable. Bachelorhood is fine, then, for several years but as a "forever" lifestyle it does leave a lot to be desired.

Cohabitation? While there is little to condemn this state, as far as you are concerned, you may just as well be married; you don't need to live with someone in order to learn more about them. Nevertheless there can be extenuating circumstances; you or your lover may be hung up by a divorce, in which case you might like to consider this as a solution with marriage as your ultimate goal.

Marriage? At heart you are a conventional character, therefore matrimony is the ideal solution for you. Try to bear in mind though that a bad marriage is worse than nothing, and that even you can make a mistaken choice. However, this is not a common occurrence among you Virgoans. You simply don't make mistakes ... do you? Of course not, you cry. But you are still not protected from divorce, as that lover of yours may well have made a mistake when it came to analysing your character. It is a thought worth bearing in mind!

VIRGO MARRIAGE CHANCES QUIZ

Answer these questions honestly and score 3 for yes, score 2 for sometimes or unsure, and score 1 for no.

1. Are you fussy with your food?
2. Are you tidy? (Ask your mate.)
3. Are you critical?
4. Have you an eye for detail?
5. Is it difficult for you to express deep emotions?
6. Is intellectual rapport more important to you than sex?
7. Do you feel that people with money problems should avoid having children?

8. Would you find it impossible to live with a waster?
9. Can you forgive infidelity?
10. Are you a hard worker?
11. Do you avoid hire purchase commitments?
12. Do you think Christmas is a waste of money?
13. Would you approach a stranger and draw attention to the fact that he has a label hanging out of his suit?
14. Do you steer clear of flamboyant clothes?
15. Would you be furious if your mate got drunk at a party?
16. Do you dislike parties?
17. Are you against living above your means?
18. When you entertain, is it possible for you to leave the washing up until morning?
19. Do you believe that divorce is frequently resorted to because the partners are not prepared to work at marriage?
20. Should large-sized families (more than 3 children) be allowed, in your opinion?

ANSWERS

1 — 30: The sign Virgo has barely touched you. Obviously you have several planets in another sign, possibly Gemini, Sagittarius or Aquarius. Read the sections dealing with these signs and you'll find yourself in there somewhere. You probably don't take marriage too seriously and you possess a well-developed sense of freedom. You can expect several marriages, but you probably need them in order to keep life interesting!

31 — 50: You are a true Virgoan and marriage is good for you. It brings out your glowing qualities. You need someone to worry about and work for and with. You should be able to make a marriage work. If you cannot, then there isn't much hope for the rest of us!

51 — 60: This is the score of a Virgoan in possession of more of the vices of the sign than the virtues. This means that life with you tends to lack fun. Try to relax more and make allowances for the weaknesses of others. If you don't take this advice, whilst you may not give up on the marriage you could find that your partner has. You have all the qualifications necessary for the deserted husband or wife.

LIBRA
(the Scales)
September 24 — October 23

Planet: Venus
Colour: Indigo blue
Partners: (In general) Aquarius and Gemini
Countries: Austria, China, Burma, Tibet
Cities: Vienna, Lisbon, Antwerp, Frankfurt, Copenhagen
Famous Librans: Julie Andrews, Oscar Wilde, John Lennon, Brigitte
Bardot, Truman Capote, Linda McCartney, Franz Liszt

GENERAL CHARACTERISTICS
As a Libran you are sympathetic, affectionate and kind. You are very
considerate of other people's feelings, and because you are so peace-
loving you try to live in harmony with your fellow man. Social
relationships are very important to you, but above all you need a
partner for true fulfilment and happiness. For this reason you are
likely to be married. If one marriage doesn't work out you will persist
and enter into another. Even when unmarried you are not without an
alter ego. You are very dependent on the approval of others. You like
to have someone around who will appreciate everything you say and
do.
    You are unusually artistic; your sense of proportion, line and colour
are superb. You vibrate towards balance and harmony and you tend
to appreciate music and other cultured entertainments where aesthetic
values are involved. You are very particular and beauty-loving in your
dress and are also very fastidious and dislike messy or dirty work.
One of your most outstanding characteristics is your love of justice
and if you feel that you have been mistreated you will go to any

lengths to oppose the wrong. Otherwise you will react to the injustice by becoming resentful and cold. When things are a matter of your own judgement you will weigh things carefully and come up with a scrupulously-considered opinion. You are, however, so subtle and finely balanced that you may tend to vacillate and fail to come to any conclusion at all. You want so much to be fair, to see both sides of the question, that it is often hard for you to decide which course of action to follow.

Because you are very considerate and sensitive to other people's feelings you may appear to be overly dependent on them. You are grateful for favours and appreciate kindness shown to you. You have critical ability, but it is constructive and kindly meant. You are very courteous and refined, good manners being important to you. You exhibit them yourself and expect them of others. You love ritual when it is tastefully done and are repelled by coarseness and vulgarity. If forced to live in uncongenial surroundings you could retire into your shell.

Librans tend to be expert in love and have distinct understanding of both the masculine and feminine roles. Their appreciation of the feelings of their partner makes sex not so much an animal passion but an art. Most Librans tend to be highly developed on the sexual plane. Certainly both are so delicately balanced between the sexes, however, that they are not distinctly either one, and homosexuality can result. You have an excellent constitution and while you may not feel exceptionally strong you have great powers of endurance and recuperate quickly from illness or disease.

LIBRA AND MARRIAGE

To you all love is sacred. If you are typical you will worship the one you love and will tend to place the object of your affections on a pedestal. You love with the mind and the spirit and are repelled by anything earthy or crude. Because you are so refined and subtle you are often misunderstood. While you can be very sincere in your feelings, you are at the same time interested in the form in which things are done. Love and courtship are very important rituals in your eyes. The Libran love cannot be chained to material expression but must be absolutely free. It would be a very unusual member of this sign who married for money or position. If this did occur you would be utterly miserable. However, where you love truly you can be offended when your love takes the physical form. You have a horror of anything ordinary or banal and can resort to perversions, not because you are immoral but, because you are so imaginative. You love harmonious surroundings and a discordant environment could make you physically ill. Beauty and simplicity are the high standards to which you subscribe. You will be charming and sympathetic to one member of the opposite sex, but anyone who offends your sensibilities will be treated to cold haughtiness, especially if they try to presume. If someone lacks attractive manners, it will not matter to you how many other virtues they possess, you will not be interested.

Bearing in mind the above, it is not difficult to imagine that marriage can be difficult for the Libran. Your list of requirements, however, is rather long and unrealistic. You would need a spouse who is as beautiful on the inside as he/she is on the outside. You would require a beautiful house in which life was always peaceful and harmonious. Children would be expected to enter the world without so much as a squeak, and in possession of all social graces. Lastly, and probably most important of all, you will expect your love relationship to remain as intoxicating and as exciting as it was on the first night you met. Quite a tall order, I'm sure you'll agree. Small wonder there are few Librans who celebrate their Diamond Anniversary. Of course, you may be lucky and your fine taste may save you from choosing an unsuitable mate in the first place. You may even be able to afford that house of your dreams. If you honestly desire a lasting relationship you will need to be a little more realistic and stop flitting from lover to lover. But then if you did, you wouldn't be a Libra.

LIBRA HUSBAND

This man can be a joy, but like the rest of us he needs the right partner to appreciate him — although if you are an independent woman who is determined to make an impression in your professional world you are advised to look elsewhere for a soul mate. Neither is Miss Practical-of-the-Year going to please, in fact; she is unlikely to raise even a glimmer of interest in him. Our Libran wants dreams and romance, not the harsh realities of life. He can make the most mundane of tasks seem enchanting. Have you ever read any of the letters he writes? Even those to the gas company or the telephone people? Or when he is complaining about services? Sheer poetry! How the confused man on the receiving end reacts is hard to say. He probably has difficulty deciding whether he is dealing with a complaint or a compliment.

Most people are bowled over by the Libran charm. Of course, there are exceptions, those who will decide that he is insipid or gushing. But such critics mostly belong to the male race. The Libran male is a woman's man. Besides, in truth, other males are jealous of his success with the opposite sex. Harmony, colour, comfort and romance are the Libran's prerequisites for marriage. He cannot cope with screaming, scruffy children, or abusive women. His wife must retain the appearance of a fashion model even while tackling the washing up. It is imperative that she genuinely enjoy those impromptu, intimate dinners during which he will woo her all over again. No point in merely tolerating him in this direction; he senses when feelings are spontaneous and is wretched if ridiculed or simply indulged. He is an everlasting Romeo and his lady must be nothing short of Juliet. When he uses the electricity money to buy her some expensive French perfume, she will begin to identify with Dr Jekyll. Does she laugh or cry? If she wants to keep him, it would be better if it were the former. This man is perhaps at his most exasperating when a quarrel starts, for he immediately senses a storm brewing — and then he becomes the invisible man. He hates disharmony and simply refuses to argue, therefore if you are the type who enjoys a good fight you can expect a good deal of frustration. On no account should his woman ever decide that he will become more sober or conservative with age. When he is seventy he will be every bit as affectionate and romantic as he was at sixteen, and just as devoted. Fortunately for him, the Libran man is never short of a mate. There are plenty of women only too pleased to put up with this kind of aggravation.

LIBRA WIFE

The Libran wife is practically identical to her male counterpart. She is all-female, and sees no reason why the honeymoon should come to an end after several short weeks. She is determined that it should last forever and, were her man ever to suggest that after two years she should learn to live through the day without him, she would be desperately hurt. The Libran ladies' man is her life. Even children play a poor second fiddle. If you are the kind of man who is irritated by telephone calls to your office during which she will declare how she loves and misses you, then you have no business to be with this lady. Chances are that she wouldn't stay if this were the case. She may appear to be unable to take a breath without your express permission, but disillusion her and take her for granted, allow romance to die and, before you know where you are, she will be gazing adoringly into some other character's eyes. Likewise he will wonder how on earth he existed before they met.

What other talents does she possess? Well, she is an adequate housewife, hardly fanatical, but as a cook she is often unbeatable — but then she understands just how much this practical talent is appreciated. As a parent she will rarely win any awards. Motherhood confuses her; remember that, despite her age, she's very much a child herself. And as a financial genius she would make a good astronaut! The Libran female really does not possess a head capable of handling all those nasty little figures. As far as work is concerned she may have a career, but it will never take precedence over her man. Should this kind of adoration worry you then you haven't the heart or the stomach for the Libran lady. But don't fret, she usually has a string of admirers, so she won't be lonely for too long.

LIBRA AND DIVORCE

The Libran's loathing of discord has frequently been referred to, therefore when it creeps into her home life the world becomes unbearable and divorce is then regarded as a necessary evil. Many

Librans divorce for reasons which may seem ludicrous to the more enduring types. The woman who had a nervous breakdown because hubby forgot her birthday, didn't comment on her new dress or missed the new hairstyle must have been a Libran! Such things are directly taken to heart and regarded as cruelty or, at the best, indifference. Add to this the sad fact that romance finally died after eight years of wedlock, and you have sufficient cause for the Libran marriage to break down. Such a character cannot be expected to function correctly and healthily without at least the illusion of a love story. Their marriage must be special, and if it begins to ail through sheer boredom, then it must be put out of its misery. What is more, the first reserve will be called in immediately those suitcases have been packed. I'm not suggesting that those born under this sign are any more adulterous than the rest of us; let us just say that Librans do not waste any time. Why, by the time the divorce has been granted our friend will already have set the date for the second attempt.

Small wonder that this sign is prone to multiple marriages. It is difficult to imagine a Libran without a mate. A lone member of this sign is not a pretty sight, for it is the sign of partnership, and those who belong to it are literally only half a person without a mate. However, the Libran's reluctance to fight can at least lead to a so-called "civilized" divorce. Instead of unnecessary wranglings this character wants a good clean fight and one of the shortest duration. Generally speaking that is exactly what they get, unless they have married someone unyielding and unreasonable. But this would be most uncharacteristic.

LIBRA EX-HUSBAND

If the Libran can be the sweetest and kindest of husbands, he can also be unsurpassable as an ex. Regrettably there are females who will take advantage of his good nature and reluctance to squabble. You know, the demanding type who wants the house, the car, the kids and the life-savings. What can he do? He sighs, sheds a few tears and hands over the lot without a murmur. He is so fair-minded that he is capable of convincing himself that the divorce is totally his fault. When he deserts his overpowering guilt, it makes him even more generous. It may take him years to recover financially. His estranged wife may be the worst shrew in the world, but please don't say so within his earshot; he will still care about her and not allow anyone to blacken her character. However, don't run away with the idea that he is a "clinger"; far from it. The Libran is quick to adapt to his new status. He will help his ex-wife adapt to her new life, but only if he is asked. When she begins dating again he will be genuinely pleased for her. It will not matter that her new lover is twenty years younger. So what? She deserves a bit of fun, he will reason with any critic: "Besides, she looks twelve years younger ..." And when he arrives to visit the

children he will be full of admiration for her efforts with them. He is
never the type to indulge in snide remarks to them, such as: "Of
course, your mother is useless without me!"

Without any doubt, there is a lot to be said for the Libran ex-
husband. He will be a friend, lover or companion on request and will
allow himself to be passed off as her brother or uncle in potentially
embarrassing situations. Furthermore, he is the original Invisible Man
if that is her wish. He is so darned obliging that she may wonder why
on earth she ever got rid of him.

LIBRA EX-WIFE

The Libran ex-wife has all the assets of her male counterpart. She will
hate to ask the erring spouse for alimony, and if she can find a way to
exist without it you can bet she will. Her friends will say she is insane
and that her ex-spouse is good for at least twice what she receives. But
she is undeterred, unless, of course, she is left with six children and no
income. Even in these circumstances she would rather manage
without his assistance if she possibly can. Nor will there be any fights
over possessions; he can have what he likes for she won't stand in his
way. At most she will be satisfied with fifty per cent of her entitlement.
Even then she won't bother if it means a fight. It's a wonder she
doesn't starve, but of course she won't. She is far too attractive:
there'll always be some man willing to bale her out of difficulty if she
needs help. So put away your handkerchief, this little woman will
survive splendidly. The Libran female may keep tabs on her ex-spouse
but only at a distance. If he is emotionally involved, she will prefer to
stay away. If not, she sees no reason why they cannot have the
occasional dinner together. While they are both free she may well ring
him at night, especially when the bed feels uncomfortably empty.
When she falls in love again, and it is usually a matter of days, the ex-
husband may think she has dropped dead for he will be conveniently
forgotten. True, once upon a time she planned her life around him, but
that is past and now she has found herself another orbit. He has
probably seen the last of her, unless something goes wrong with the
new love, when she may return in order to plant a few tears on his
shoulder. The departed husband may have found the Libran woman
an impossible wife, but she will be difficult to resist as an ex.

LIBRA AND THE COMMUNE

The only possible explanation for Librans joining a commune is that
they harbour some romantic illusion about this life. And no doubt
they will stick around while that illusion remains intact. But once it is
shattered, the Libran will disappear; such a way of life has little to
recommend it to members of this sign. Bear in mind the fact that the
Libran dislikes hard or dirty work and possesses a notoriously lazy
streak — hardly desirable in this set-up. Remember too that
appearance is desperately important. One can imagine the sort of

remarks the Libran might be subjected to when he or she decides to dress up for dinner, simply because they feel like it. No, Libran nature is such that it cannot tolerate tough and ready manners or surroundings; it has to be first class all the way. And why not, if you can get it? Anyway, there is no reason why you shouldn't try, is there?

LIBRA AND COHABITATION

The Libran's need for constant romance could well be filled within this type of arrangement. Just think of it ... six months with one love until the romance fades, and six months with another, and so on. There is only one problem. The Libran's inability to fight does not mean that his/her mate suffers from the same deficiency and if this is the case then our friend will want out. However, some members of the human race become quite distraught when an affair ends. And at the first sign of unpleasantness the Libran will withdraw any statement in an effort to calm the not-so-beloved lover, who may be forced to stick around for ages unless a foolproof way of breaking it off can be found, one which will ensure that nobody gets hurt. And don't forget, this could become a necessity every few months. This doesn't mean, on the other hand, that cohabitation is out; but the relationship will need to be worth all this aggravation. Otherwise bachelorhood could be the only way open. However, all Librans will tell you that freedom has its disadvantages; when love strikes, they must be with the revered one. A night here or there is insufficient. It is all or nothing.

LIBRA LOVER - MALE

Married or single, this character possesses all the qualifications of the perfect lover. He charms, coaxes and romances his love. Nothing is too much trouble or too good for her. He never tires of singing her praises and has been known to write the occasional poem to her charms. He will never take his woman for granted and, while devoted or obsessed by her, he rarely suffers from jealousy. This is not a Libran vice. It may be that he realizes she will not find a lover any more attentive than he; but he overlooks the fact that there are other Libran lovers in the world. Because of the absolute trust placed in his love he is totally deflated when betrayed. He may not rant and rave like a demented soul, rather he will quietly pack his bags while nurturing a broken heart, and move on.

But what of the relationship if it is successful? Initially they may not have discussed marriage but, to the Libran, to stand up before the world and declare their love and their intention of sharing the rest of their lives together is the ultimate romantic experience. There is only one thing more romantic and that is the patter of tiny booties. "I yearn for something just yours and mine, darling," he murmurs. But be warned, he will cool considerably under the wails of a bellowing baby. And then there are the nappies — they may be just too much! Only if you can retain that poised and elegant image while changing the baby's rear end should you consider a love child with this character. Many Libran marriages miraculously come to an end about one year after junior has been born. And that year will have been the longest of his life, you can depend on it. So you must be well prepared before setting up home with this individual. Mind you, if you can cope you will not regret it.

LIBRA LOVER — FEMALE

That admirable young woman who cooks the roast in her bikini? Can she be the same one who invariably changes into something sheer and seductive following dinner? Yes, she can be. Her name? Miss Libra of course. Sounds perfect, doesn't she? And she is, provided you are willing to be placed on a pedestal and worshipped. If this behaviour embarrasses you, then, believe me, you cannot live with this lady. She may call you "Sugar Plum" over the telephone, "Sweetums" in front of your rugger pals and send little love notes to the office. If you ask her to refrain, you will break her heart. She may be sixty but, she is a sixteen year old at heart when it comes to love … and don't you dare forget it. No doubt you believe that she is made from fine porcelain but she is not so fragile as she looks. Therefore, if you feel the time has arrived for you to part then you must tell her so. Naturally, she will be upset. But within a week you will see her on the arm of some hunk, gazing up into his eyes. Yes, she is a marvellous lover, but run for cover when she becomes broody and begins to talk about presenting you with a little pink bundle. Her love child could turn out to be just the opposite, love-less. She will hate the baby if it ruins her figure, she will resent the fact that there is never enough time to pretty herself up, and she will despair when she is too tired to make love. If you find yourself tempted to give into this whim, find yourself an experienced nanny; it could save your relationship and find her quick. Now … to marry or not to marry? Well, be warned: that Libran lady is habit-forming. Once you have adapted to her funny little ways and tasted the fruits of her love it will be difficult for you to imagine life without her. When you arrive at this stage it is only a matter of time before you pop the question. So … if you set up home with this lady be prepared for a march down the aisle.

LIBRA CHILD AND DIVORCE

If you have a Libran child, especially a girl, then I bet she is blonde, blue-eyed and dimpled. So gentle and sensitive, you no doubt believe; and, of course, to a point, this is correct. But no matter how dependent and adoring she may be with her parents, should life make it necessary for her to make do with only one of you she will adapt. Libran children healthily react instantly and spontaneously to the break-up of marriages. But once those tears have all been cried, the next thoughts are for her parent, the one with whom she must live. You thought she was an angel before, but you ain't seen nothin' yet! She will redouble her efforts to please, not wanting to be a burden on you, but she will not cling like her sister Cancerian. There are however several don'ts to be observed.

She must never bear witness to quarrels between parents. She is quick to sense tension, so that won't do either. If you cannot bear the presence of your erring spouse then arrange to be out when he calls. And never expect her to take sides. She will see all sides to an argument and you will tear her in two if you demand her loyalty and expect her to come out against the missing parent. No matter how diabolical he or she was, the Libran child will always see something good there. Maybe the erring father did fool around with other women, beat his wife and was clearly off his head; to the Libran child, no one was funnier or more witty. He could certainly play a convincing cowboy or Indian! So you see, you cannot win. The Libran is naturally fairminded; take a leaf from their book.

LIBRA CHILD AND REMARRIAGE
Libra being the sign of partnership, this child instinctively understands your need for a partner in life. Even a young Libran appreciates the need to share, and fully realizes that this also applies to Mummy or Daddy. As far as this child is concerned it is an inescapable fact of life. Provided he/she is not expected to abandon the missing parent then serious problems should not arise. And never lose sight of the fact that the new parent means someone else to share with. This child is not selfish, and in fact cannot be truly happy in any activity unless there is someone else to participate. Where discipline is concerned, justice needs to be the key word. The sooner the Libran child decides that the new parent is a fair-minded person, the sooner love will begin. But woe betide the bully or male or female who simply issues commands without fair explanation, for in such circumstances the Libran child will grow rebellious, lazy, careless and impossible. But generally this child is easy to love and to manage, therefore, if you are having any problems, chances are the fault lies somewhere in yourself.

CONCLUSION
We have taken a brief look at the Libran in various relationships. Now ... which is the right one for you? Well, actually each has something to offer. Let's recap.

The commune is strictly out, if you are a typical member of this sign. If you have any romantic notions about this way of life you are doomed to disappointment.

Bachelorhood? Highly satisfactory for a while, for a couple of years or maybe between marriages. The single state can be fun and will permit you to have as many admirers as you can manage, but eventually you will want to share your life with another person. You are not a natural born loner, and at this point you may try ...

Cohabitation — clearly feasible for the Libran, but if the relationship is successful then it is certain to lead to marriage. Marriage is then the ideal, but only if you can be more realistic. You may be attracted to the idea of growing old with your love, however, you must be prepared for that love to change and develop. There are few people who have the ability to live in a constant state of romantic bliss. Should you locate one, though, you could just make the Darby and Joan Club! As a Libran, never kid yourself that you can lead a free and independent life, it is not your style. Lonely Libra is unhappy Libra. You need other people. But most of all you need love ... and lots of it.

LIBRA MARRIAGE CHANCES QUIZ

Answer these questions honestly and score 3 for yes, 2 for sometimes or unsure, and 1 for no.

1. Are you indecisive?
2. Is it difficult for you to say "No"?
3. Do you fear a monotonous marriage?
4. Is love the prime reason for marriage?
5. Is life without romance inconceivable to you?
6. Do you believe that there is someone for everybody?
7. Does parenthood worry you?
8. Are you sensitive to surroundings?
9. Are you always well dressed?
10. If the house were to catch fire, would the possession you grab be an item of clothing?
11. Do you like very masculine/feminine partners?
12. Are you sentimental?
13. Were you in love more than three times before the age of twenty?
14. Do you believe money is valueless unless it is used to give pleasure?
15. Do you loathe sports?
16. Are you miserable when not in love?
17. Do you put on weight when your love life goes wrong?
18. Is it difficult for you to separate love from sex?
19. Is it hard for you to·remain faithful?
20. Do you invariably quarrel with your mate or partner?

ANSWERS

1 — 30: Libra has only touched you very gently. You must have other planets in Scorpio, Capricorn or possibly Taurus. Read these sections and learn more about yourself. You may not be the flighty type but your marriage could get into difficulty through sheer boredom. And if it does break down it will be you who is deserted.

31 — 50: You are a typical Libra, but fortunately you possess most of the better characteristics of this sign. You need a romantic mate and if you find one your marriage may last. But you are sure to make at least one mistake. Therefore two marriages are predicted.

51 — 60: You are a typical Libra. But you possess more of the faults associated with this sign. You ride on a constant search for novelty and pleasure. Marriage will either evade you completely or you will experience several divorces. Watch out ... you could end up very lonely indeed.

SCORPIO
(the Scorpion)
October 24 — November 22

Planet: Pluto
Colour: Deep red
Partners: (In general) Cancer and Pisces
Countries: Norway, Catalonia
Cities: Valencia, Dover, Halifax, Liverpool, Newcastle, Washington, New Orleans, Milwaukee, St Johns
Famous Scorpions: Picasso, Robert Louis Stevenson, Maria Antoinette, Robert Kennedy, Richard Burton, Petula Clark, Rock Hudson, Prince Charles, Billy Graham

GENERAL CHARACTERISTICS
You are extremely forceful and exhibit tremendous strength of will. Your compelling personal magnetism fascinates other people. Whether or not you are good looking is of no importance, this is a sign par excellence for sex appeal. There are two distinct types of Scorpio: the higher, or noble type, represented by the lusty, soaring eagle, and the lower type, represented by the snake or scorpion. The latter types are formidable adversaries, which is evident in their personal appearance. In better types the expression may be stern but the disposition is kind; in others the countenance can almost be ugly, but with a compelling attraction for the opposite sex.

Higher types have an unassailable integrity. Devoted and high-minded, using their ability to dominate people and situations for the universal good, they are unselfishly dedicated to the advancement of all mankind. Lower types are sly, secretive and cunning with diabolical passions and uncontrollable jealousy, underhanded and treacherous. When they feel they have been offended, they lust after revenge. They fly into a rage at the smallest provocation and are dangerous opponents, taking advantage of any weakness and resorting to any means at their disposal, however unfair, to cause injury. They are totally vindictive, having neither scruples nor compassion for human suffering.

Those of you who are Scorpions are generally shrewd and energetic, persistent and capable of hard work. You are indefatigable in the pursuit of a tangible goal or ideal, persevering and tenacious where others would fall by the wayside. For this reason you can be outstandingly successful, although the chances are that you will have to fight uphill all the way. But you always use your wiles and wits to defeat rivals; you are cool and deadly. Your very subtlety coupled with strength and the will to work are wonderful qualities for science and medicine. Crime detection may also be your forte, although the lower Scorpion may make the most dangerous and wily criminal. The ability to keep secrets, dissimulate and deceive is excellent for undercover agents and spies. Domestically the Scorpion can be something of a tyrant. If you do things his way he is relatively peaceful; heaven help you if you go against him. He is easily offended and will not rest until the wrong has been avenged. The Scorpion is never mistaken in his own eyes and never brooks the slightest dissent.

Scorpions love passionately, more so than any other sign in the Zodiac. In the higher types it is a noble emotion; the lower types are immensely selfish and possessive. There is a gross sexual appetite as well as over-indulgence in food and liquor and, once aroused, jealousy is all-consuming. In religion, self-righteousness and bigotry combine in you. Although they are usually prolific, most Scorpions are too domineering to make the best parents, for they impose their wills relentlessly on their offspring. There are two types of women who come under this influence. One is possessive and highly sexed, shrewd and scrupulously jealous. The other has immense willpower, ambition, high ideals and determination. The lower type is revengeful and treacherous when thwarted, the higher type, while admirably has the courage of her convictions, is determined to have her own way. With a male, the woman in his life will be either of the types mentioned above. He himself may be passionate and so strongly sexed that he throws his life away on ruinous associations with women.

Scorpion powers of observation are phenomenally sharp and accurate, and having conceived an idea you do not rest until you have transformed it and given it to the world at large.

SCORPIO AND MARRIAGE

You can be passionate, emotional and strong-willed, or else you can be lax, sensual, throwing your life away in the pursuit of pleasure in every form. But when you love, you love intensely, and in the physical sense, and are so wilful that you tend to go to extremes. If someone does not return your love you dislike them completely; even if they do reciprocate, your love life is bound to be stormy. You expect the object of your affections to surrender completely and abjectly to your will. Few people are willing to put up with this once the initial fascination passes. You are very straightforward, but you may be so direct that you frighten the person with whom you are in love. You must try to be more tactful and reserved.

You are possessive and jealous and you must guard against excesses of feelings. Love may give rise to jealousy in the initial stages, but soon jealousy is all-consuming and your desire for revenge is implacable. Many people, however, find you magnetically attractive. You can be sensual and earthy, and no matter how much you give expression to your animal desires you can never really satisfy them. Most Scorpions overdo it when it comes to sex. In many cases, because of your environment and training you may repress your instincts and experience frustration and discontent as a result.

Needless to say, the regular heartbreak that accompanies bachelorhood is not for you. You deliberately seek marriage, although you are not about to settle for just anyone. You recognize your mate on sight, and that is that. Of course, this is when the problems can begin. "What problems?" you may ask, since you do not realize just how difficult you are to live with. No doubt you disagree, so try reading the previous paragraph again, I think you'll admit that you are not an easy bundle of love for anyone to take on!

SCORPIO HUSBAND

Not an easy person to please. If you are freedom-loving, flirtatious and fiercely independent, then you need the Scorpion husband like you need another head. The career lady may be suitable, but only with certain provisos: she will need to take holy vows which will, in effect, state that she undertakes never to be more successful than he, or better financially rewarded. It is this character who gave voice to women's liberation in the first place. Equality? The nearest his wife will come to that is when in bed with him, and even then it's debatable. Yes, ladies, you must be prepared to live in his shadow. It must be his prerogative to take the important decisions, he who pays the bills and instigates love-making. Furthermore, he is always right, he has never been known to make a wrong move, not one that he will admit to anyway.

Naturally, then, he veers away from the divorce courts, for such a state of affairs will mean confessing failure, or at least a lack of judgement. Unfair, you say. Possibly, for he does possess some sterling qualities, but they will only be noticeable to the right lady. For example he can be Mr Faithful himself, usually out of fierce passion, but occasionally out of sheer perversity. To him adultery is only resorted to when he has been able to accept that his marriage has failed. But this in turn is tantamount to acknowledging that his choice of wife was at fault. He is also possessive and jealous; what is his is his and heaven help anyone who tries to take it from him. However, he is an excellent provider and protector, although in close contact some may feel, quite justly, claustrophobic and smothered. Sexually speaking — well, he could successfully take on a bedful of girls if he so desired, but this is not his scene. This man has difficulty with the expression of deep emotion, and sex is often resorted to for this purpose. So the physical act must mean something, akin to love and worship, not: "There's nothing on TV tonight, so let's get on with it."

When the Scorpion man becomes a parent he is a good father but a severe one. All too often he attempts to impose his own will and beliefs on his offspring, so that in time he is faced with a full-scale rebellion. And if he is typical he can be totally unyielding. Clearly he needs a woman who shares in his beliefs, but one weaker of will. There cannot be any fight for domination in this household. He is the master. Better accept this fact or quit. Furthermore, his mate will need to be attractive, highly sexed, at least willing to learn in sexual matters, but most important of all, she must be devoted and loyal. Life is never easy for this man, and as women become more and more independent so his problems increase. Neither is he the type to shop around. He sees what he likes and it is instant Rudolph Valentino. Commitment is then made, despite the fact that the poor girl may be kept hanging around for years before he finally decides the time is opportune to tie the knot. Any reluctance to do so usually stems from his intense ambitions. He wishes to fulfil himself or, at least find his way. Responsibility is not treated lightly. Bear in mind that responsibilities are taken on for life with this man, therefore· he needs understanding when he repeatedly postpones that big day.

Lastly, although he may be difficult, once his heart has been won his love is certainly worth having. His lady will never feel unsure or insecure again, with this strange magnetic character to protect her.

SCORPIO WIFE

The Scorpio wife is, perhaps, just a trifle easier to live with, but otherwise she is similar to her male counterpart. She is ambitious for herself and for her man, and he had better live up to her expectations. She will happily skimp and save while he makes his way to the top, but if he lets her down, or, worse, refuses to try, then heaven help him. No one is as unhappy as an embittered female Scorpion. Her man can say goodbye to peace and tranquillity; that is, until he leaves. However, to be just, it must be emphasized that she is unlikely to marry a loafer or loser in the first place. She will make darned sure that he has the right qualifications before taking him on. Once the knot has finally been tied, he would be wise to forget the rest of the opposite sex. She will be faithful to him and naturally expect him to reciprocate. This female is the most passionate and jealous in the Zodiac. The mere suggestion of an alien perfume will be sufficient to send her screaming back to Mother. Would be Don Juans, please note!

On the credit side, the Scorpion woman is a boon to the right hubby. She is sexy, elegant and magnetic, a delight at social gatherings, and will do anything to further his career. She will work hard for him and her children, but she will not tolerate any nonsense from either quarter. She needs respect, love and complete devotion and probably in that order.

The Scorpion's critical and penetrating eye must not be overlooked. It is imperative that she never be subjected to lies, no matter how ingenious. There is little point. It is a racing certainty that she will know before the first word has died on your lips. However, this sixth sense will also tell her that her man is ill, worried, insecure or in need of her. She can, invariably, provide instinctively what is needed, with the possible exception of freedom. No one in their right mind should ever trifle with her; she has a long and retentive memory and never, never foregoes her revenge. Rather she will wait patiently for an opportunity, and then quickly strike with full force. Remember, she is a Scorpion, and therefore behaves accordingly. So, my friends, this isn't a lady for the faint-hearted. YOU HAVE BEEN WARNED!!!!

SCORPIO AND DIVORCE

Divorce is relatively uncommon among members of this sign. In the first place, as previously mentioned, the Scorpion finds it difficult to admit to a mistake; and secondly, those razor-sharp perceptions endow members of this sign with the excellent ability to judge other people. Therefore, they rarely ever choose an unsuitable mate. However, assuming that divorce is pending, then the experience will be far from pleasant, for failure is a blow to the Scorpion ego and pride. It also acts as matchwood to a keg of dynamite. Whether the Scorpion leaves or was deserted, there is one thing of which you can be sure: it was not done peaceably. There is a violent temper lurking behind those beautiful eyes; it may not ignite for months on end but, when it does, watch out. Even when the battle is over and both parties have gone their separate ways, this is by no means an end to matters. First, wherever possible the Scorpion will hold up legal processes and, with the use of a modicum of ingenuity, the delay will run into a couple of years. Bear in mind that the Scorpion is similar to the elephant in that he/she rarely forgets. Not surprisingly, then, divorce leaves an unpleasant taste in this character's mouth, together with a thirst for retribution. You can be certain the Scorpion will vow never to attempt the experience again, and in many instances this is a vow which he manages to keep.

SCORPIO EX-HUSBAND

Logically there must be some pleasant Scorpion ex-husband. Those with other influences on their personal birth chart; but we are discussing the die-hard typical individual and frankly I'd rather keep a tiger than have an ex of this sign.

Instead of accepting the divorce as an unfortunate necessity, this character becomes vengeful. What he fails to comprehend is that he is making himself just as miserable as his victim. This does not mean he will attempt to dodge his financial responsibilities, but he will make it as difficult as possible, and may even insist on dropping the weekly or monthly cheque around in person. If she has any sense at all, she will not permit this, for once he puts a foot over the threshhold he will be impossible to budge. To expect to remain on friendly terms is unrealistic. A considerable amount of time will need to pass before he can accept the fact that she no longer belongs to him. And, in the meantime, he will persist in his attempts to run her life. Ideally, he should be denied the chance, though naturally he will want to visit the children, so the course of life will become complicated. In this instance certain measures are advised. His ex-wife must ensure that a friend be present when he arrives: a witness or a protector, if you like. The best cure for him is a new love, and if this character is really creating havoc then perhaps she can assist matters in this direction.

Better face up to it, while he is free he will do his best, or worst, to ensure that his former partner remains unattached too. A wise Scorpion would, just for once, make life easy for himself and put that ex-wife right out of his mind, preferably never to lay eyes on her again. This done, he must first attempt to make a completely new circle of friends for in this way there will be no memories. Next step is to accept all invitations that are offered, together with any willing females. Understandably, it will not be easy for a man who has been faithful to one lady for years to suddenly realize that he is at liberty to bed-hop. Ideally he should plunge into an affair as quickly as possible. This may make things seem more painful, but once it has been done he will feel like a new man and notions of revenge, which must be self-destructive, will slip out of his head. Then and only then will he be ready to begin his new life.

SCORPIO EX-WIFE

If as a Scorpion you seriously believe that you can make a better job of being an ex-spouse than your brother Scorpion, then think again. You are just as capable of mean and spiteful behaviour, yet where's the point? That man may have made you unhappy and had the temerity to desert you, taking with him the best years of your life ... but hold it right there. How can you be certain that they were the best years? It could be just the reverse. The best years may be just ahead, if you can refrain from glancing over your shoulder and focus those beautiful eyes in the right direction. Are you honestly stating that you couldn't be attracted to another man, because your ex-husband was totally your idea of perfection? Come on. If that were true, you would still be with him, or would have made certain that he didn't want to escape. I do hope that you are getting the picture.

Age isn't that important. There are just as many twenty-, thirty-, forty-, and fifty-year-old men as there are women. So get out into that big world and find one, two or three. No one is suggesting that you leap feet-first into remarriage; it will be some time before you are ready to take that step again. But a few practice runs could be in order. Possibly your morale may be at an all-time low. You could well feel too deflated to take the initiative, but if your ego is in bad shape, do something about it. Go about rebuilding your confidence. Most Scorpions have incredible eyes, so why not experiment with some new makeup, a visit to the beauty shop? And if you can afford it, take a holiday, some new home décor or a party. Any or all of these will pick you up and prepare you for action once more. If you are determined to be self-destructive then of course no one can deter you from wallowing in self-pity and growing fat with frustration; but, remember, you will only be hurting yourself. If you seriously believe that your erring spouse will die with concern, you have got to be joking. You are divorced now, right? He pays you alimony doesn't he? And possibly child support. OK … slash your wrists if you must. He might manage a few tears, but he will soon smile again as soon as he remembers you have saved him quite a bit of time and money, not to mention aggravation. So, you see, this is not the answer. You have the chance to start a new life, grab it with both hands and go!

SCORPIO AND THE COMMUNE

All right, so you picked yourself up and went to the commune. I hope you are satisfied. It is not really your glass of whisky, is it? No doubt you have already offended everyone in the establishment while attempting to help or suggesting changes that would suit you better. No, my friend, you have made a mistake. Communes are for independent, generous, hard-working souls, not for sophisticated, proud and possessive Scorpions. In actual fact the Scorpion would be a darn sight happier in the army, so why not try the Foreign Legion? It would be about as suitable and as desirable as the commune for you.

SCORPIO AND COHABITATION

Scorpions who have just suffered a painful and tough divorce may find this alternative to marriage is an ideal solution. It will provide time in which to discover whether or not there is the courage to live with another person again. Obviously the never-married Scorpion will also consider cohabitation as a way of life. But those born under this sign are usually extremists: it will be marriage certificate or marching orders! The Scorpion is not a puritan, but he does not see the point in setting up home unless it is to be done properly. Of course, he/she is happy to spend a few nights with this lover and a few nights with that, but this is hardly cohabitation. Returning to the divorced Scorpion — even you will eventually feel that wedding bells are necessary. Those born under this sign prefer an ordered and legal existence. Everything neat and tidy. Besides there is a tendency to worry about what the neighbours might think. Nevertheless the Scorpion may set up several homes before locating the member of the opposite sex who can tolerate these little quirks. If cohabitation offers any advantages, then, it is as a trial period only, during which time the lover can decide the ability to put up with this character for life. The Scorpion is unlikely to enter such an arrangement half-heartedly or because it is *the* thing to do. Trial marriage is invariably the sole motivation behind this state.

SCORPIO LOVER – MALE

Despite the fact that the Scorpio man is passionate, loyal and determined to achieve, this does not help him to become the best person in the world to live with, especially outside of marriage. His biggest problem is jealousy. Initially he may be able to stifle small misgivings and insecurities but only for a limited period. When his lady declares that she will return from work at six, then it had better not be half-past, or even a quarter past, the hour, otherwise she will be greeted with a torrent of accusations. The Scorpion also has other drawbacks. He is intensely critical and often destructive. He recognizes a lie when he hears one, no matter how grey. In fact there are only two colours in his spectrum, black and white. So the more disillusioned by his lady love he becomes, the more he will tend to lose himself in a bottle. When provoked he can actually become violent, and it doesn't take much to incite him.

So rule number one when taking on this character is to be one hundred per cent honest. Rule number two is to always be tolerant, despite his intolerance, otherwise escape. On the optimistic front, when he believes that he can place all his trust in his woman then there is none more content and devoted, but bear in mind that when he is unhappy there is no one more impossible. If the relationship is successful then he will be spurred on to greater heights. But he will never neglect her. The moment he downs tools, he will rush home to be near his lady. She will probably have more love than she can handle. But, remember, a love affair with a Scorpion means travelling over a thorny road and it takes a tough and determined female to survive.

SCORPIO LOVER — FEMALE

Imagine a lady with the determination of Amy Johnson, the looks of Elizabeth Taylor and the temperament of Mount Vesuvius ... Great! Now you are prepared for the Scorpio female. If you are really lucky then you may not actually see the volcanic aspect to her, although you will always sense that it is somewhere within her. If you are spared this experience, this means that not only is she crazy about you but also you are playing a straight game of love with her. Provided you continue along this wise course, life will be free and lovely, you may even marry and both live happily thereafter. But try any double dealing and you'll discover in record time that you have picked the wrong lady. Logic and reasoning are to no avail; the fact that everybody is doing it makes her see red, white and blue. She is only concerned with your life together and what you are both doing, the rest of the world can go hang! The trouble is, despite her faults she is quite irresistible, isn't she? With her smouldering eyes and the sensual figure — why, you could promise her everything. But please refrain from doing so, unless you are prepared to keep your word, otherwise you will have a life full of aggravation. The fact that you are both unmarried is of no importance: you are hers and she is yours, and if you cannot subscribe to this you should move on. Although you will find it impossible to find a love which burns as fiercely as her or for as long, this lady needs plenty of reassurance without the security of marriage. Therefore, if you are having problems with her, you are simply not giving her enough love. It is as straightforward as that. Caress her and she purrs, ignore her and she will bite your leg in order to get attention.

SCORPIO CHILD AND DIVORCE
In this instance, while much depends upon age, the younger the better, there is no point in kidding yourself that life is going to be easy. No way will you ever convince this child that erring Mummy or Daddy is anything but a paragon, so don't try. There are two rules which must be observed with the Scorpion child. Expound upon your mate's virtues but do not exaggerate. (What do you mean, he doesn't have any virtues? That isn't nice!) And rule two: get the two of them together as much as possible. In fact it is yourself you should be worried about; be prepared, for eventually this child will recognize both parents' weaknesses, and this will happen earlier than it would with another child. The young Scorpion has a penetrating eye that sees all, knows all and will certainly need no help in this direction. It won't be long before he/she is criticizing you and your life, and when this does happen, gently draw attention to the child's own faults and those of people close. It will be understood that everyone cannot be expected to be perfect. This child has a sixth sense, so truth should be your keyword. Once he or she has reached the age of comprehension. Tell a lie and you will be interrogated until you are hopelessly lost in your web of deception. At this point it would be goodbye to your relationship with the Scorpion child. However, do bear in mind that just as he or she is able to sift facts from fabrication, so is he or she able to discover and appreciate your finer points. Furthermore, while

remaining loyal to that unworthy creature to whom you were married, young Scorpion will be equally loyal to you in spite of everything. The Scorpion child and divorce may be incompatible, but with your honesty and love you will both survive, even though *you* may doubt it at times.

SCORPIO CHILD AND REMARRIAGE

Some children love everyone; young Scorpio does not. You belong to a very exclusive circle if you have this child's devotion. Therefore, try not to be too disappointed if your youngster takes one look at the new parent and decides that it is instant hate. Admonishment will only make matters worse, so keep quiet and cool. If you are experiencing problems, then jealousy is likely to be at the root of them. Life will only be eased if the new parent is of the opposite sex to the child, for in this case they will not be seen to be a rival. The Scorpio child is well aware of the sex difference; this you will discover when you observe your offspring flirting with the new member of the family. But you can expect the worst if the new Mummy or Daddy is of the same sex as the child.

In this instance the new parent is seen as a clear threat. Only when satisfied that he/she will not be deprived of love and attention will the child begin to relax, but whatever you do, don't rely on friendship devloping, not for some time anyway. The intruder — for that is what the new parent will appear to be — will be analysed, observed and criticized before emotions are allowed to seep into the relationship. And even then this will not occur if the child decides that the new partner is unworthy of its adored parent. Should this happen, it will be everlasting and instant war. The child will never relent, and life will be impossible if you take sides. Matters may even reach the point where you think of saying goodbye to number two. There is really only one way — the new parent must measure up to the child's expectations but not against the missing mother or father. The new parent must be accepted for himself or herself, not as a replica of someone else. You would be wise to decide before marriage whether the two of you can get on, otherwise you can be sure that the Scorpio monster is quite able to prise you out of the house. Handle children of this sign correctly, patiently wait for their friendship and, later, you may receive their love. When this happens, they will still stand by you. In other words, if the Scorpion likes you, you are in — otherwise forget it. He or she won't change, on that you can depend. This child can be adorable and trustworthy, or an imperfect monster. Feel your way carefully and keep your fingers crossed.

CONCLUSION

Of the various relationships contemplated on the previous pages, which one is ideal for the Scorpio? If indeed anything is. Bachelorhood is not really your can of beans. The typical member of this sign is simply not made from Don Juan material, or the female equivalent. Naturally, you may take time to find that elusive soul mate of yours. But your love and sex life, in the meantime, would hardly make enthralling reading for readers of Playboy. And what do you do when you do finally find your soul mate? Set up home together in order to give it a whirl? Not your plan of attack. If you are honest, as most of you are, you will admit that your jealousy would never permit this state of affairs.

So ... what do we have left for you? Right third time. Marriage. It may leave a lot to be desired for some, but for you it is the only answer to a sane existence. However, try not to have a nervous breakdown if you are past thirty and feel as though you are forgotten; you are naturally discriminating and, as already stated, bad ex-spouse material. So take your time, otherwise you could make a lot of people unhappy, including yourself.

SCORPIO MARRIAGE CHANCES QUIZ

Answer these questions honestly and score 3 for yes, 2 for unsure or sometimes, 1 for no.

1. Are you jealous? (Ask your mate.)
2. Do you believe in "marry in haste, repent at leisure"?
3. Do you believe that ninety per cent of all divorces are unnecessary?
4. Are you against Women's Liberation?
5. Do you believe that today's children lack discipline?
6. Do you believe that fidelity and marriage go hand in hand?
7. Would it be impossible for you to forgive an unfaithful mate?
8. Would you fight for a principle?
9. Are you ambitious?
10. Would you expect your children to do well in life?
11. Are you fiercely independent?
12. Is sex important to you?
13. Do you lose your temper easily? (Ask your mate.)
14. Are you critical?
15. Are you an excellent judge of character?
16. Do you bear grudges?
17. Is it difficult for you to make friends?
18. Have you keen likes and dislikes?
19. Are you stubborn?
20. Does sex need to be an expression of love?

ANSWERS

1 — 30: You are an open-minded, free-wheeling character, perhaps a bit too much so. You do not basically believe in the "one man, one woman" syndrome. In fact you are unlikely to expect a relationship to last overly long and are, therefore, not ideal marriage material. You need a relationship that allows you plenty of leeway. Scorpio touched you lightly. Your individual chart probably reveals several planets in Sagittarius or Gemini.

31 — 50: You are a typical Scorpion, but fortunately you possess more of the virtues than the vices attached to this sign. You are not easy to live with, but then what Scorpio is? You have all the qualifications needed for a good husband or wife. Marriage is important to you and you will put everything you've got into it. Your chances of success are good.

51 — 60: This is the score of the typical Scorpion but one who has most of the vices of this sign and few of the virtues. You believe in marriage and will work at it, but unless you become less unyielding and opinionated you are the type who will be deserted, and maybe not just once.

SAGITTARIUS
(the Archer)

November 23 — December 21

Planet: Jupiter
Colour: Light blue
Partners: (In general) Aries and Leo
Countries: Spain, Hungary, Madagascar, Australia
Cities: Toledo, Stuttgart, Budapest, Cologne, Nottingham, Bradford, Sheffield
Famous Sagittarians: Walt Disney, Mark Twain, Sir Winston Churchill, Dick van Dyke, John Osborne, Jane Fonda, Paul Getty, Sammy Davis Jnr, Beethoven

GENERAL CHARACTERISTICS

You are high-spirited, impetuous and refined. You resent coarseness in others and are a born aristocrat in your tastes and tendencies. Your attitude is normally bright and cheerful. You are also capable of great brilliance and daring. You are bold and brave, uncompromising in your love of freedom and you grant everyone the same right. You are very democratic, having friends in all areas of life. You like the people around you to express themselves freely and you speak your mind with great independence; at times, you can be too direct and blunt. Your intuition is unbeatable. If you go against your natural hunches and inclinations it can hold you back from the very actions that would, ordinarily, bring you success. Normally you have high ideals and true vision, your greatest luck in life comes from trusting yourself. You are also very trustworthy; your integrity is above reproach. You would be embarrassed were someone to doubt you and you are also very thin-skinned and easily humiliated by the smallest slight. You are, at the same time, both proud and shy. You tend to mix sporadic effort and a variety of things, rather than applying yourself to one project. Once you have put something down it is hard for you to begin working on it again. You do, however, have great presence of mind in an emergency, and often what brings you to the fore is the way you solve situations and have to reason unexpectedly.

You love discussion and you are able to convert others to your viewpoint by holding a dialogue. You are usually an amusing conversationist, and whilst you may be sceptical about some facets of religion you are, nevertheless, very philosophical, at the same time being unorthodox in your beliefs. In business you take a direct approach and are usually financially successful. However, you do not like routine work and are bored by petty details. You love the outdoor life, especially sports such as hunting where dogs, horses and shooting are involved. You are very active and love to run or to ride and usually you love the races. You are not particularly earthy and have an aloof attitude towards physical functions as if, by your ignoring them, they will go away.

Sagittarius rules the thighs, hips and tendons, so you may suffer from troubles from these parts. You are also highly strung and under stress you can be subject to nervous breakdown. Generally, though, you are healthy, and this is the best sign for living to a ripe old age.

SAGITTARIUS AND MARRIAGE

For you, sudden attractions usually turn into long friendships. You are very loyal once you have entered into a friendship. Instant attractions to the opposite sex are not always fortunate, however. Your choices are often so impulsive that they do not work out and broken engagements and marriage often result. Sagittarian men are true bachelor types; even after marriage, they cannot tolerate restraint. They are not in the least domesticated and can become selfish and difficult to live with. They may also be critical and sarcastic with relatives they have reason to resent, or a spouse who has bored or disillusioned them.

If a woman, you will be idealistic, ethereal and refined, and will attract the highest types — when it comes to other women, that is. But they will not be envious or antagonistic towards you. You will have few, if any, enemies among women. You will act with exquisite sensitivity in your relationships with the opposite sex; you are both gentle and shy and would never appeal to a coarse or common man. In the case of a man, the woman in his life will resemble the preceding description. He has to be careful as to how he approaches them for they are so timid that the slightest misstep will cause them to flee from him. However, while the woman's sensitivity and high spirits may appeal to him, he cannot be relied upon to attend to down-to-earth matters the way a Taurean or Virgoan male would. This man is like a shooting star, brilliant but impermanent. He lacks warmth and the power to sustain emotions. He often attracts someone who has ordinary passions, only to disappoint them by failing to respond. He may therefore seem cold or fickle. But because he is high-minded and refined he demands these qualities in the object of his affections. If he finds a lack of idealism and pride he immediately loses interest. The slightest indelicacy or flaw will put him off for ever. As most human beings have some defects it may be impossible for him to find satisfaction. This is not true in friendship where Sagittarians display the highest degree of loyalty and affection. You exhibit a certain detachment, separating the physical love from the ideal. You could never be successfully matched with anyone gross or earthy. In love you must be absolutely free; a conventional relationship would be banal. If someone tried to tie you down you would be bored and take the nearest avenue of escape. Only the most subtle and intense ploys will attract you. But your usual disillusionment and inconsistency account for the fact that many of you remain bachelors, faithful to no one but your ideal.

If you are a woman of this sign then you are delicate and equally elusive. You have no more desire than the men to sacrifice your freedom for the sake of love. Although there are obvious exceptions to this general rule, Sagittarius and marriage are rarely compatible. Should you ever take this fateful step it will need to be with someone who is happy to keep a very loose rein on you. The slightest tug will cause you to break free and disappear over the horizon.

SAGITTARIUS HUSBAND

Just because you actually managed to drag, coax or blackmail this character into walking down the aisle doesn't mean you can now relax and expect him to behave. If he is typical to his sign then your problems could be just beginning. It will only be a short time before you realize that he has no intention of giving up his precious freedom, for anything or anyone. However, to do him justice, he will allow you the same latitude, although he is unable to advise you on what to do with the kids while you are out enjoying yourself.

Needless to say, while the family is young you are going to know exactly how the Prisoner of Zenda felt! Meanwhile your Sagittarian husband attends a rugger, tennis or cricket club. When it is not sport that keeps him from you it will probably be politics. A union meeting perhaps, a debate of some description which cannot function without him. But do not complain, it could just as easily be the blonde who works in the local bar, or the redhead who recently moved into the district, and in some cases it will be!

All right, you say you'll forget about having children — then what? Are you prepared to stand in sub-zero temperatures while he supports his local team? Or sit for hours listening to him orate, debate or protest about anything at a political gathering? Our friend certainly needs a very special lady, one totally independent, free from jealousy and prepared to spend a good deal of time alone. Some kind of arrangement is clearly needed. The "you go your way, and I'll go mine" must have originated with the Sagittarian. Indeed, it may well prove satisfactory, but again I ask — for how long? Possibly forever, if both parties can remain devoted to each other while living separate existences, otherwise the chances are relatively slim. Eventually, one of these free-wheeling characters is going to collide with someone who has more to offer than sex or the possibility of a challenge. When this occurs it could be the end of their relationship, their arrangement and their marriage.

Assuming that you are the perfect mate for this man, and have been able to hang on to him, then he has various assets on his side. He will always be active, interesting and aware. He will allow you to keep your individuality and will be the first to congratulate you when you are promoted over his head. He is also sociable and fun-loving, but be warned. Keep an eye on that budget — your Sagittarian man will certainly not. He cannot be bothered to waste his time on financial problems. He will insist that he has more important things to hand, and he probably has. Just check that one of them isn't a blonde! If it is, ensure that you are the type who can take it.

SAGITTARIUS WIFE

If you imagine that the Sagittarian lady is any less sporty or politically motivated, just because she is a woman, then you couldn't be more wrong. She has the same virtues and the same vices. Her man needs to be one hundred per cent behind Women's Liberation while at the same time striving to ensure their roles aren't totally reversed. It could happen. If you want this little lady, then be prepared for at least a 50/50 arrangement on everything, right down to Junior's potty training! Otherwise you will be courting disaster. Furthermore, it is not wise to display possessive or jealous tendencies. She will remain yours provided that she doesn't feel those chains. Immediately she is made aware of them, she will break loose. The Sagittarian wife should possibly be retitled "The Sagittarian chum", for this describes her perfectly. She is not a drudge, nor a seductress, but a friend. If you want anything more you had better look around for a very different type of female.

SAGITTARIUS AND DIVORCE

Although you may not be exactly wild about the prospects, neither will you be filled with horror, disgust or foreboding. Your one regret is likely to be that you have failed, have actually taken on a challenge that did not prove to be mastered by you. Without having any figures to confirm the following statement, I am convinced that most Sagittarian divorces are caused directly or indirectly through the seeds of discontent which are sown or instigated by feelings of restriction. The breakdown of your marriage will only strengthen this trait, and you will wish to remove the fetters as quickly as possible. No long-drawn-out legal battles for you, if it can be avoided. Not that a piece of paper will prevent you from feeling completely free, you understand. Inside your head you were divorced the minute you both decided to split up. The rest is a mere formality.

A divorce may be the end of the world to more intense types but, to you, it is yet another experience and one from which you will bounce back with relative ease. You Sagittarians usually like to taste and embrace life as a whole and this includes some of the more unpleasant aspects of it. That wonderful sense of logic you possess will save you every time, on that you can depend, Sagittarians are survivors — and don't you forget it!

SAGITTARIUS EX-HUSBAND

You may not be of the stuff that great husbands are made of but when it comes to the title of "ex-husband" then your nearest rival is probably a mile away. Naturally enough, you do possess one drawback — namely your unreliability in connection with finances. If you are sincere when you innocently proclaim, "I wish to remain friends and will never allow you to starve," do try to remember the weekly cheque! You should also try to control a tendency to moonlight all over the countryside without telling her. If you can overcome these tiny flaws in your personality you could qualify for the "Ex-husband of the Year" award, otherwise you may well walk away with the award for "Louse of the Year".

This problem solved, you are Mr Wonderful, more like a big brother or an old friend than an ex-husband. You'll sympathize when her lover removes his toothbrush from the bathroom, escort her to the occasional social function when she is unable to find a suitable partner and may even organize the reception should she marry (that is if her new man is foolish enough to allow such goings on). It almost goes without saying that you will be delighted to supply her with a night down memory lane should it be required. The appropriate word to describe you is — I believe — accommodating.

SAGITTARIUS EX-WIFE

When it comes to taking bows for being an ex-spouse you should be quite exhausted. You may even surpass your male counterpart. Financially speaking you like to be independent, therefore if it is at all feasible you may forgo the alimony altogether. If not, your demands are at least reasonable. As far as the personal side to your relationship is concerned, outsiders may hardly notice the change in status, unless one of you is emotionally involved elsewhere. You will continue to support all your ex's activities, even to the point where you will, as usual, supply tea and refreshments for his cricket team. You will also give him advice on his sex or love life should these hit the rocks. Should he remarry, you will be the first to volunteer to paint the bedroom in his new house while he is away on honeymoon. Why not, you ask? Well, the problem is that the world is not full of open-minded Sagittarians, there are also one or two possessive Scorpions and Taureans, not to mention the occasional sensitive Piscean or Cancerian who will severely criticize such behaviour. However, you never were the type to care or listen to what others are saying about you. Therefore, if all parties are agreeable, then why not?

SAGITTARIUS AND THE COMMUNE

This mode of life was probably instigated by a Sagittarian. It meets with your needs perfectly; furthermore, if your life lacked meaning before, this could well be the answer. The commune will certainly help you to fill the gap. The humanitarian within you will abruptly surface and you will be working and striving towards the common good. No task will be too lowly or unimportant, the members of the community will have no problems too irritating or petty to require your attentions. The commune will also allow you to spread your wings. If you enter it with spouse and family in tow there will always be someone to babysit. If you enter alone you will be surrounded with friends and yet be free to come and go as you please. It takes a special person to make a go of this way of life, and that person could very well be the Sagittarian.

SAGITTARIUS AND COHABITATION

Next to you remaining permanently single, there cannot be a more suitable alternative. One problem, though, exists. Just make sure that a desire for matrimony isn't lurking behind those irresistible eyes, otherwise the ants will have arrived at your picnic. And, naturally objectives will need to be identical if peace is to be retained. But whatever your intentions, state them in your usual candid manner; it will save you a lot of trouble later on.

Do not assume for one moment that you are going to get everything your own way. Remember, it is as easy for your lover to dispose of you as it is for you to get rid of them. Also bear in mind that while being unmarried may save you a divorce if the relationship fails, this doesn't mean that you will escape unscathed altogether: a jealous lover can cry, swear or threaten just as effectively as a jealous spouse. Of course, if you are happy to drift from relationship to relationship then you will have no problems at all, neither will you have emotional contentment. But, then, Sagittarians are not often motivated by their emotions. Therefore this kind of existence may just work for you.

Lastly, the trial marriage should be considered. This is an excellent idea if you are a typical member of this sign. Cohabitation will help you decide whether or not you could live with what you may well describe as restrictions. Naturally enough, it will also assist your lover in deciding whether the unsettling affect you bring into his/her life is acceptable.

SAGITTARIUS LOVER — MALE

If you like a life full of activity and surprises then this could be your man. Provided, that is, you have been unable to locate a jealous bone in your body, not even a little one. If you are domesticated, passionate and intense then, lady, you had better get quickly away before he walks all over your sensitive heart with hobnailed boots.

The word lover is inappropriate in this instance, not that I wish to insult his sexual prowess, the fact is that he rarely has the time. No doubt, if he did, he would show the other male members of the human race a few tricks, but regrettably he is far too busy. The Sagittarian loves people, they fascinate him. Furthermore, he has an ever enquiring mind and because of this your moments alone with him will be few. The only thing any sensible girl can do is accompany him; if she doesn't someone else is sure to. Therefore, if you are living with this individual because he makes you laugh, interests you and is a good friend then you are on the right lines. However, should you worship the ground he walks on, love him for his beautiful body, you have taken a wrong turning somewhere.

A last word of advice: this is a frank and honest man, perhaps to the point of extreme. Remember, if he tells you at the outset that he is not interested in matrimony then you had better believe him. It will save you some heartache if you are secretly hoping for eventual marriage.

SAGITTARIUS LOVER — FEMALE

Now gentlemen, use your imagination. It is Sunday and you have been engaged in some hectic sporting activity and you have developed a raging appetite. You arrive home full of anticipation, sit yourself down and grab your knife and fork. Suddenly, your Sagittarian lady appears and announces that she forgot to light the oven. Do you swear, say "Oh, dear, oh, dear!" or laugh? Now, let's be honest! And how would you react if she told you she had given your beautiful dinner to the needy family down the road? Still laughing? Good! For you could be just the man for this female. Any other reaction indicates that you are in for a rough time. This is not a suitable woman for the "pipe and slippers" character. She is unlikely to possess a domesticated bone in her entire body. She might play at it occasionally, but improving her mind, body and world are more important.

In some instances even earning a living may seem to be higher up on her list of priorities than you. She won't play Juliet to your Romeo, of that you can be sure, so there is no point in expecting it. Fortunately for her, and contrary to popular belief, the world is not populated with men who are totally ruled by their emotions, or their sexual needs. And if you should happen to be one of them, you are in with a fair chance of success with this lady.

SAGITTARIUS CHILD AND DIVORCE

There can be few children who are actually delighted when parents split up, and the Sagittarian child is no exception. Nevertheless, recovery is sure to be quicker than for most. You could have a considerable problem if the break has necessitated a move to a smaller house or flat, as this could mean that the child has to share a bedroom. If this does apply you will no doubt already have decided that your child is a selfish, materialistic brat. But hold on ... all is not what it appears. We have returned to the Sagittarian's dread of restriction. The larger house is not required in order to show off to the neighbourhood kids, it is needed solely for the purpose of having somewhere to feel free, room to move and to grow. If this is not possible, you may have a full-scale rebellion on your hands, but try not to despair.

Sagittarians do not enjoy their childhood, for such a state demands that they accept a modicum of discipline, together with a life which is controlled, for the most part, by others. Natural and right, you may think, but not to a Sagittarian. Therefore, you should relax and stop tearing out your hair! This child of yours is simply aching to grow up. Oddly enough, the Sagittarian child is fairly mature at an early age, but an immature adult.

SAGITTARIUS CHILD AND REMARRIAGE

This little character is candid and honest with you; the least you can do is to be just so with him. It is far better that he learns of your plans for remarriage from you rather than a friend or acquaintance. And if he should demand your reasons, simply explain and with honesty, unless of course you are after your fiancés money! Emphasize the word "friendship" and do minimize gushy sentiment or behaviour. The child is perfectly able to understand that you need a friend and supporter, preferably someone you also happen to be in love with, but emotional outbursts or declarations of any description are totally beyond comprehension.

The new parent should remain enigmatic for a while, for the Sagittarian child cannot be indifferent when his/her curiosity is aroused. Ideally the new relationship should not be rushed. It needs to develop slowly and naturally. Obviously matters are helped considerably if the child genuinely likes the new parent. In this case problems will evaporate, at least until the new parent finds it necessary to mete out some discipline. This is the testing point for, handled the wrong way, the relationship will deteriorate as quickly as it developed. There is absolutely no need to walk gingerly around the child's emotions as if they were made of porcelain; provided you have a well-developed sense of justice, allow as much freedom as is feasible and offer a passive love, then this is all this little character will need in order to survive. Bear in mind that Sagittarius is the sign of the survivor, therefore your problems should be minimal.

CONCLUSION

On the previous pages we have looked at the Sagittarian in various relationships and now is the time to recap and sum up. By now it should be fairly obvious that the typical Sagittarian is not ideal marriage material, therefore if you are searching for Darby and Joan you are going to be disappointed. But, there again, if you are, you are not a true Sagittarian. Marriage is perfectly acceptable to you if you can get accustomed to the fact there may be more than one.

Cohabitation is certainly worth a try, but you'd be wise only to contemplate it with someone similar to yourself. Opposites may attract in some instances but not in yours.

Now to consider the commune. Such a lifestyle may also fulfil a need at some juncture in life. You are nothing if not adaptable. However, ideally, bachelorhood is the state you are naturally born into. You are not the type who will ever be lonely; people cluster around you constantly. This applies from babyhood to old age. Naturally you will make your own decision but I hope this chapter has helped you to inspect your own failings objectively.

SAGITTARIUS MARRIAGE CHANCES QUIZ

Answer these questions honestly, and score 3 for yes, 2 for sometimes or unsure, and 1 for no.

1. Do you suffer from claustrophobia?
2. Could you accept remaining permanently unmarried?
3. Does domesticated bliss bore you stiff?
4. Do you prefer your admirers to come in numbers rather than one at a time?
5. Would you prefer the whole world to be your home rather than any one country?
6. Do you believe that undying love went out with Romeo and Juliet?
7. Do you find jealousy hard to understand?
8. Do you loathe emotional outbursts?
9. Do you enjoy studying and learning?
10. Do you believe that fidelity in marriage is over-emphasized?
11. Could you forgive a faithless lover?
12. Are your paternal/maternal instincts dormant?
13. Do you enjoy the company of your own sex as much as that of the opposite?
14. Are you rebellious?
15. Do you have a keen sense of justice?
16. Do you believe in polygamy?
17. Are you tactless? (Ask your mate.)

18. Are you physically active?
19. Do you believe that sex is over-rated?
20. Does intensity of any description bother you?

ANSWERS

1 — 30: Sagittarius may have touched you but it is hardly noticeable. It seems likely that you have several planets in Virgo or Capricorn. No doubt you will have discovered that much in the previous chapters do not apply to you; you are far more practical and domesticated than the average Sagittarian and, as such, your marriage chances are increased.

31 — 50: You are typical of your sign, fortunately with more of the good characteristics than the bad. You are a delight to know and the best friend anyone could ever have. But as a spouse you leave quite a lot to be desired. You will certainly marry, possibly more than once — you are too attractive to escape for long however clever you may think you are!

51 — 60: This is the score of a typical Sagittarian but one who has more of the faults than the virtues. Your sense of freedom is blown up out of all proportion and is nothing short of sheer selfishness. In fact if you have any sense you will stay well clear of the marriage scene. You are doomed to be disappointed otherwise.

CAPRICORN
(the Goat)
December 22 — January 20

Planet: Saturn
Colour: Green
Partners: (In general) Virgo and Taurus
Countries: India, Afghanistan, Mexico
Cities: Oxford, Delhi, Mexico City
Famous Capricorns: Humphrey Bogart, Cary Grant, Howard Hughes, Joan of Arc, Martin Luther King, Mao Tse-tung, Richard Nixon, Edgar Allan Poe, Ava Gardner

GENERAL CHARACTERISTICS

You have a towering ambition. Like your symbol the Goat, you leap over both adversary and obstacle in your climb to the top. Indeed, you have all the attributes to succeed since you are hard-working, reliable and have tremendous initiative and drive. You are both cautious and conservative, with a deep respect for authority. You have your own preconceived notions of what is right and wrong and are stubborn in upholding them. You tend not to be particularly original or creative but stick to tried and true methods. This may limit your horizons and make you less adaptable to changing circumstances than you ought to be. At best you have a healthy amount of self-respect and are deeply moral, although the weaker Capricorn may have the less desirable trait of being obnoxiously self-righteous, certain in your own mind that you have always done the right thing at the right time and in the proper way. Indeed, you take life seriously and have a strong sense of duty. You are very willing to assume responsibility, in fact, you seek it out, although later you may complain about how many burdens have fallen upon your shoulders and how much more than anyone else you have done. This is true from the time when you were very young. And you are very steady, faithful and conscientious in the extreme. When it comes to money, members of Capricorn are usually thrifty, but some of them can be miserly with their cash. They can be trusted to make sound and conservative investments and will account for every penny, but they are not likely to be brilliant speculators, usually being too concerned with conserving small amounts to think in terms of making a great coup.

You express yourself dryly in speech and writing and may tend to make classical allusions. You are not likely to sacrifice yourself for others or to give yourself utterly in a relationship with the opposite sex. Basically you are too self-centred and self-interested. Certain aspects to your Sun can make your sexual appetite rather gross, though you are rarely subject to perversion. You have an iron constitution and terrific powers of endurance. But recurring depression can make you want to drown your sorrows and in some cases may give rise to chronic alcoholism. There is a certain coldness in your make-up, and your self-sufficiency makes you a somewhat solitary soul. You tend to fix all your hopes and fears on one ideal, about which you can be obsessive, so much so that your imagination plays tricks on you. This results in false illusions and can lead to despondence when things fail to go your way. At best you are likely to look on the dark side of things, so guard against brooding over disappointments and becoming dispirited and gloomy.

You accept the relatives you were born with and the circumstances of your life as a matter of course; you usually operate within the hereditary framework and rarely choose a path very far afield. In many ways you tend to feel that what was good enough for your family is good enough for you. You are alert and eager to learn, possessing the ability to make quick decisions, look at a problem and resolve it in a split second. And still be quite correct!

Women of this sign are very practical and want everything to be as they have planned. While not being particularly warm or sympathetic they are dependable and made of the sternest moral fibre. Other women are generally not well disposed towards the female Capricorn; even if they are, she is often of more benefit to them than they are to her. The male Capricorn tends to attract women of the above description, who though they will be faithful are not likely to contribute to his happiness. He may remain a bachelor or else women will play a subsidiary role in his life.

The good or higher Capricorn types can lift themselves above their moods and work doggedly to achieve great ambitions, whereas the lower types allow themselves to wallow in despair, complaining of their failures while doing little to alter the situation.

CAPRICORN AND MARRIAGE

You may develop an interest in the opposite sex later than the average person, but you form strong, permanent attachments when you do. Sometimes your interest in sex is altogether submerged under other concerns. When it comes to animal pleasures you can be lusty yet at the same time detached. A good deal of your energy may be given over to the quest for a good time, but you can be very small-minded about it, expecting the other person to comply with your wishes completely. You can be selfish, expecting much more of others than they are willing to give. You can be jealous and touchy and very particular about other people's attitude towards you. Because you are afraid of being refused, you are inclined to be suspicious and you expect the other person to make the first move. Once you are sure of being wanted, you then feel confident enough to commit yourself, but you need every encouragement before you can relax and love. You want to possess your loved one totally and to have him/her respond by being even more enthusiastic than yourself. As long as intimacy lasts you are perfectly content and act decently. You are, however, very proud and should you feel rejected, you can instead of being warm and demonstrative become antagonistic and withdrawn. Happily settled you are faithful and domestic; you prefer staying at home to going out socializing.

As a parent you are often too domineering with your children, tending to squash their desire for self-expression. You are not inclined to be especially affectionate in your behaviour and should guard against being too strict and unyielding in discipline with a high-spirited child. Because of your inborn respect of authority you should also guard against a tendency to tell your child that the teacher is always right, whether he is or not.

Like all of us, one person will bring out the excellent qualities in your nature, while another will incite the bad, although in your particular instance there is a larger gap between the two. A happily suited Capricorn will always do his or her best for loved ones. No matter how unkind life may be, you will fight for survival more determinedly and effectively than any other sign. With the wrong person, however, you are capable of becoming a tyrant, a martyr — both of which will be combined with a persecution complex. In these circumstances you are impossible to live with. And, in such a situation, your marriage must inevitably break down.

CAPRICORN HUSBAND

The concept of the "pipe and slippers" man must have been dreamed up by a woman with a Capricorn husband, for it suits him admirably. However, you could not be blamed for believing that this is an ailing breed. This is not strictly so. True, he may have traded in his slippers for a pair of platform shoes but rest assured they will not be as outrageous as his contemporary's, in fact you may have trouble deciding whether they actually qualify as platforms at all. As for the pipe, you can be sure that he will not have exchanged it for anything as outlandish as an earring! Besides, the Goat is probably a business man, therefore, he would look somewhat ridiculous dressed like a pop star in the office or bank. Unlikely to lead to promotion, one would have thought! And you can be certain that he is chasing promotion, for this individual is extremely ambitious. When you consider his dependability, practicability and ambition, you have some promising husband material. However, certain flaws in his personality often mean that the right lady remains elusive. There are occasions when his depressive and pessimistic tendencies need a light-hearted influence, a woman who is able to see the funny side to the gloomy picture he creates. Conversely she must not be too crazy, or irresponsible, for she must impress his boss and work colleagues, while also managing to adhere to the rigid family budget which he will no doubt draw up. Furthermore, this mythical Miss must be ambitious, although not for herself; such fine feelings need to be reserved for her man. Emotional and/or highly-sexed ladies need not apply for his hand in marriage! Not that I wish to cast aspersions on his sexuality, you understand; it is simply that, for the most part, our friend is too busy pushing his way upwards to allocate any time for such frivolous behaviour.

The Capricorn husband can be as mean with his time as he is with his money, and that can be really stingy. Now that his faults have been paraded for all to see, it is only fair that his virtues be given an equal airing. Do you need a man who will protect you from the nasties of life, especially the financial ones? Do you find it hard to cope with pressure? Yes? Then you should run to our friend, he is a veritable tower of strength. For sheer guts and determination this is the strongest sign of the Zodiac. His wife can be certain that whatever it is he wants from life he will achieve it, no matter how long it takes, and it can take time. But the Capricorn husband does not expect an easy life, therefore he remains undeterred. Needless to say, he is a good reliable father, although somewhat serious. His wife may have to draw his attention to the folly of expecting too much from the children. Apart from this, there will be small reason for complaint, providing she fits the above requirements. If not, she will be in for a difficult time.

CAPRICORN WIFE

Having this female in your corner can be likened to walking through a dark alley with Muhammed Ali. Protection is her forte. No one can really hurt you with her by your side. Furthermore, you will have the confidence to surpass even your wildest professional dreams. Like her male counterpart she is fiercely ambitious for her loved ones. On their behalf she will unobtrusively kick, scratch or bite anything which stands in the way of their success, which is fine if they really desire a trip on the road to fame and riches. Otherwise this ride will become somewhat bumpy. If your only ambition is to lead the simplest, easiest or laziest life possible, then you have no business becoming involved with this lady. She is, of course, able to appreciate a rural scene with Mother Nature at her most flamboyant, but she is soon going to wonder whether there is gold, silver, tin or oil in them thar hills! She will not chastise her husband if he cannot match the Aga Khan diamond for diamond, but he must at least try. When he has failed there will be no recriminations; she simply transfers her ambitions to her son, daughter, or possibly herself.

The Capricorn lady believes that just as time or money should not be frittered, neither should life. To drift would be her idea of hell. She needs to know where she is going and with whom. I may seem to have likened her to a bludgeon that her husband can utilize to threaten or beat about the heads of rivals or opponents. But this does not make her any the less a woman. The Capricorn wife is usually extremely feminine and elegant and her taste is impeccable. She may have been raised in a slum but you would never guess it. She polishes herself as she does her ambitions. However, sex and ambition are often incompatible, therefore the sexual side to marriage can have its problems, for like her brother Goat she is frequently too busy to take time out for relaxation. Her physical needs diminish when this occurs. Her idea of a nightmare husband is a scruffy, lazy, unattractive, unambitious sex maniac. However, while it is true that she may fail to notice her man dying from sexual starvation little else escapes her, for she can provide anything that is needed to pull him through any kind of problem.

CAPRICORN AND DIVORCE

Fortunately, the fact that Capricornians are late developers can save them from experiencing a divorce. Even so, this sign is often opposed to marrying. Either they never do it, or do so more than once. Saturn rules Capricorn and is thought to be a most unlucky planet by some astrologers, although many, including myself, tend to think of this planet as a disciplinarian. Members of this sign sometimes need to work a little harder than their fellow men. When marriage starts to fall apart they drift into one of their notorious depressions, and while it lasts they are incapable of seeing anything good or beautiful in the world at large. Life is a disaster, they are a disaster. Needless to say, as long as this attitude persists one can hardly expect much progress to be made on the legal side. Letters remain unanswered, phone calls ignored. Then, just as friends are surrendering all hope for his survival, the Goat surfaces full of fight and determination. It is almost as though while escaping in their despair they had been recuperating in some way. Once this metamorphosis has occurred then legalities are pushed through in record time.

Work is effectively used as a refuge and under such circumstances Capricorns throw themselves into frenzied activity. This serves a double purpose: it keeps the "blacks" away and takes the mind off the empty house. The Goat may be lonely but isolation does not go to waste. Why, before you know what has happened, in the process of exorcising that erring spouse they have reached the top of their profession. Some people may take to drink, others to drugs, but the Goat takes to work. At least by doing so they are guaranteed the alimony and legal costs.

CAPRICORN EX-HUSBAND

Your value as an ex-husband depends upon whether you are a good or bad Goat. If you are the hard-working type or you fall quickly into a new relationship, then you are excellent. Bills and alimony are all paid on time and you keep well away from your ex, unless you are asked for assistance or advice. If you are a bad, or lower Capricorn, then oh, dear. What a woeful sight you are! You may be unable to afford the alimony but you'll pay such a convincing poverty-stricken role, one worthy of an academy award, and be so realistic that you'll end up believing it yourself. On top of this, self-pity will ooze out of every pore and much of it will drip all over the erring spouse. She may be gracious and put up with you for a while but, sooner or later, she will want you out of her life. When she does, she will become immune to the tears on her new carpet and the hang-dog expression. This may occur when she finally embarks upon her first affair. It is perfectly natural for a newly divorced goat to feel depressed and lost for a while, but do try to keep such a mood within the bounds of reason. Be realistic: anyone with a depression which is sustained longer than a few weeks is in trouble and needs help. Try to be philosophical and dust down your determination. You are a fighter and you are honestly trying to tell the rest of us you'll never find another female attractive? That your ex is the epitome of womanhood? Come off it! You would have made darned sure that she didn't want to leave you had this been the case. Before you can start a new life you'll need to look objectively at the old one, otherwise it is not inconceivable that you might make the same mistake all over again.

CAPRICORN EX-WIFE

This Capricorn woman is very like her above brother. If she is a good or higher type then she will throw herself into her work or children and make a million plans for the future, none of which will include the ex. But, if she is a bad or lower Capricorn, then apart from her depression she will become an unpleasant money-grabber. Give her the opportunity and she will bleed that ex and his bank manager white. She wants the house, the car and every penny he earns whether she needs it or not. She is too busy feeling sorry for herself to make any effort towards her own financial outlay and upkeep. No, he must pay and if he is at all soft in the heart, or head, he will pay, and pay and pay. Naturally she will be feeling down, especially if he deserted her; that is enough to deflate any girl's ego. But if there isn't an attractive man around to build her up, she will have to do it herself.

The Capricorn female needs a goal to work towards. If she has gained weight, as so often happens to married women, then she must set herself a reasonable target weight and diet. A couple of elegant dresses in the coveted size will act as a wonderful incentive. Any change in appearance will improve morale, and a new image is definitely called for if you are feeling inadequate. Should this not apply then, as with brother Goat, it is work, work and more work. Eventually you will meet someone else but you are not a bed-hopper or a simpering lady who cannot exist without a man in her life, any man. If you are typical of this sign you would rather do without than flutter your eyelids at some idiot. The golden rule with you is — allow plenty of time.

CAPRICORN AND THE COMMUNE
Your natural ability to work hard will stand you in good stead if you decide to adopt this life style, although the other members of the establishment may not be prepared to tolerate your black moods. However, you may be too busy to be self-indulgent. Strangely enough, despite your ambition, you can usually adapt to a spartan existance and endure the harshest of conditions, although prepare at some point for that ambition of yours to resurrect itself and push you off and out once more into the materialistic world. In the meantime the commune could well see you over that difficult patch in life.

CAPRICORN AND COHABITATION
Cohabitation can be a success for the mature Goat, and maturity, as you no doubt realize, has little to do with age. A kid in this instance can be a Capricorn under the age of thirty, and maybe older. Members of this sign are acutely aware of the sex difference and find it impossible to be themselves when there is a member of the opposite sex around. Consider this, together with the fact the Goat desires the approval of others, and you have an individual who will adopt this lifestyle purely to impress others with what a wag he or she is!

Such a Goat is not only a danger to prospective lovers, of which there will be a long string, but also to himself or herself. Conversely, mature Goats will behave and treat this life quietly, for his/her own benefit and not that of an audience. The Capricorn is ideally suited to such a life. Our friend loves and cares for the lover, but is always practical, not swinging on a chandelier or making promises it may not be possible to keep. In fact, such a Capricorn is probably unimpressed by marriage, perfectly able to function in an adult relationship without being consciously aware, or unaware, of a piece of paper. Provided that this character can find a partner likewise inclined then no problems should exist.

CAPRICORN LOVER — MALE

If you have managed to get your hands on an adult, higher Capricorn then hang on. He is worth his weight in uranium. It doesn't take a gold ring to make this character faithful, or to make him slave away on your behalf. In fact, if you are compatible, then years will fly past before you have had a chance to do anything about that missing marriage certificate. If so, then you may both agree to stay as you are.

One of the advantages that the married status is supposed to offer is to make one feel secure, but, ladies, you don't need a marriage for this, all you need is a Capricorn man. He is all the security any woman could ask for. And if a third person should ever come between you, then it will not be his fault. He may be a notorious flirt but he really cannot be bothered with the dramas involved in running two love affairs at the same time. Not unless he is a lower Goat. This type may remain in your heart and your flat for approximately three months, and what a gloomy period in your life that will turn out to be. When he has sapped your last drop of energy, convinced both of you that you are his body and soul, then he will be off. How can you distinguish between the good and the lower? Relax, it is obvious. Observe their behaviour for a couple of days and the truth will quickly out.

CAPRICORN LOVER — FEMALE

This lady also comes in two separate packets. First there is the "Why aren't you more successful — whine, whine — more attractive and sexy — whine, whine — more wealthy — whine, whine" type. This no doubt attractive lady sits on her perch with her palm permanently outstretched. Her lover could work twenty-four hours a day, every day and maybe even earn enough to buy her the occasional mink, take her to the ball three times a month. But would she be satisfied? Would she, hell! If you find yourself lumbered with this little package may I suggest, good sir, an ejector seat for her next birthday present.

Then, of course, there is her higher sister. She too is ambitious for position, success and material comfort, the difference being that she will either settle for what she feels her man can accomplish comfortably or lend a helping hand. She does not nag, she considers, plans and suggests. She may sometimes fall victim to depressions but she keeps them to herself and does not behave like a spoilt brat. It is easy to separate these types: the former tends towards ostentation, the latter invariably displays excellent taste.

Sexually speaking, the former is never satisfied and doesn't hesitate to say so, while the latter happily adapts to her man's appetite, whatever it is. As far as marriage is concerned, the lower lady will expect it in a pretty parcel like everything else, whereas her more mature sister will be quite happy to leave the relationship as it is, perhaps in the secret belief that if a change is made devotion may evaporate overnight. Therefore, before you cohabitate with a Capricorn lady make certain that you have the Jekyll and not the Hyde.

CAPRICORN CHILD AND DIVORCE

Your Capricorn child may look somewhat wistful and forlorn, but underneath that exterior lurks a determination to survive anything you or life can hand out. You can expect your little Goat to sink into a depression but do not become neurotic about this, unless it persists for more than a few weeks. All Goats, good, bad, young or old, can be depressed at times, and for the most part do not need a logical or tangible reason. So relax, they will not become manic depressives overnight. Once the black clouds have rolled away you will notice a brighter face, but he or she will adopt a cooler attitude to you and your erring spouse. But, it too, is another phase and once it has passed you will be surprised at just how adult the child has become in spite of those tender years. For now he/she will begin to worry about you. Try to contain your surprise when you suddenly find yourself seriously discussing telephone bills with, to all intents and purposes, a mesmerized six-year-old. You may even be tempted to reveal the real reasons for your marriage break up in its entirety. But, "Mummy and Daddy fell out of love" is all that is necessary in this case. This child then is perfectly able to handle the situation. So put away the tranquillizers, you will need to do a great deal more than become divorced before you turn him into a juvenile delinquent.

CAPRICORN CHILD AND REMARRIAGE

Just as our little friend was able to cope with and adapt to divorce, so will the child adjust to your remarriage. But, please, do not spring it as a surprise. The "Guess what you're having for Christmas?" approach will not only accelerate the aforementioned depression but prolong it. Give the child and the expected parent time to get acquainted before dropping the bombshell. Even then the news should be broken as casually as possible. Remarriage needs almost to seem inevitable. Therefore, the more you can make it sound as if it were always understood, the easier it will be accepted. Once the depression lifts, you may find the young Goat a little frosty for a while. But don't draw attention to it and the thaw will come in its own good time. Be on your guard if the child is jubilant or sweetly reasonable, for this spells danger. Chances are you have hatched out a lower type Goat who has quickly calculated the best way to play off one parent against the other for material gain. No point in searching those oh, so blue eyes for evidence of this fact; it will soon arrive in concrete shape. However, if your Goat belongs to the higher herd then acceptance will come slowly but surely. And you cannot force the pace — therefore don't try.

CONCLUSION

You may be a Capricorn who personally experiences all the various relationships discussed on the previous pages. Or maybe you will be lucky and find the ideal life style or partner on your first attempt. Only a look at your personal birth chart can reveal this particular secret with any certainty. Let's take a look again at the relationships with the typical Capricorn in mind.

First, never lose sight of the fact that you are a late developer and, if you insist on an early attempt at marriage you are destined to be disappointed. Marriage can be ideal for you but you change and develop one hell of a lot between fifteen and twenty and yet again from twenty to twenty-five. Your chances of finding matrimonial bliss are therefore increased with the number of wrinkles you possess. Neither is it ever too late for you; if you wish to marry at seventy, go ahead. You should have finally matured by this time and if you aren't then, let's face it, you just aren't going to make it.

The same can be said of cohabitation. You can be too immature but not too mature. These two relationships tend to merge into one as you grow. A Capricorn may marry a lover if made to see that it will somehow make life easier. But you will certainly not take this step for purely emotional, romantic or sexual reasons.

Life in a commune can also be a good exercise for you when you are recovering from a broken marriage or are, generally, without purpose to your life. But you are too ambitious to make it a lasting lifestyle.

Lastly, bachelorhood. It too serves its purpose while you are growing up. But you are not adept at handling the Don Juan kind of existence and you could end up the most unpopular bachelor boy or girl in town. You prefer one relationship at a time, one you can explore, learn from and grow with before you move on. This will be repeated several times if you are a wise Goat before you are ready to decide whether to marry, cohabit or join a monastery/nunnery! As I said, the later the better, so don't give up! you've plenty of time.

CAPRICORN MARRIAGE CHANCES QUIZ

Answer these questions honestly, and score 3 for yes, 2 for sometimes or unsure, and 1 for no.

1. Do you suffer from moods during which you feel utterly hopeless?
2. Would you dearly love to be the much-admired man or woman about town?
3. Are you a worrier? (Ask your mate.)
4. Are you a hypochondriac?

5. Would you postpone marriage until you felt financially able?
6. Do you need a regular wage packet?
7. Are you a social climber? (Be honest!)
8. Are you ambitious?
9. Are you calculating?
10. Are you stingy with money and possessions?
11. Do you believe in marriage?
12. Do you care what others think of you?
13. Would you prefer to sacrifice your sex life and give up any professional achievement?
14. Do you have reclusive tendencies?
15. Are you over-indulgent?
16. Are you a defeatist?
17. Do you enjoy gossip?
18. In your opinion, does marriage need children?
19. Does flirtatious behaviour get you into trouble with your mate when attending parties?
20. Are you a snob? (Again, be honest!)

ANSWERS

1 — 30: This is hardly the score of a typical Capricorn. Pisces or Libra play an important part on your birthchart; read the appropriate chapters and you will see what I mean. You are easy-going, perhaps to the extreme, and could very well drift through life professionally, materially and personally. You may, of course, make a happy marriage if you meet someone strong enough to get you together. In the meantime cohabitation would be the wisest way to go. Unless you want your marriages to run into double figures.

31 — 50: This is the score of the typical Capricorn. You possess, fortunately, more of the virtues of this sign than the vices. Provided you remain single until your mid-twenties you have an excellent chance of making a success of marriage. You are not the type who gives in easily. You certainly won't allow a wedding band to beat you if you can cure its problems.

51 — 60: This is the score of the typical lower Capricorn, one with the vices of this sign and very few, if any, of the virtues. Probably, you will try to outdo Henry VIII in the number of your spouses. You may be attractive, but others find you grasping, selfish and whining. You are hard to take. Thank your lucky planet that the block was abolished and replaced by divorce or you wouldn't have lasted twenty-four hours in the married state.

AQUARIUS
(the Water-bearer)
January 21 — February 19

Planet: Uranus
Colour: Electric blue
Partners: (In general) Gemini and Libra
Countries: Russia, Poland
Cities: Hamburg, Bremen, Salzburg, Brighton, Stockholm
Famous Aquarians: Charles Dickens, Lord Byron, Shelley Berman, Abraham Lincoln, W.C. Fields, Mia Farrow, Ronald Reagan

GENERAL CHARACTERISTICS

You are noble, moderate and sound. You believe in helping others and while you can be generous and self-sacrificing for your fellow men you do not go to extremes. You do not like to see anyone suffer and will go to any lengths to avoid this. You have an instinctive understanding of human nature, coupled with great tolerance for the weakness of others. You know that the mistakes people make in the normal course of life are for their soul's growth and therefore for their own eventual good in the larger scheme of things. Your own character is usually well-balanced and strong.

You are scientific and love new inventions and discoveries; you may even be an inventor or scientist yourself. Your powers of observation and ability to theorize often amount to genius, and you are a profound student of human behaviour. You believe firmly in the brotherhood of man and in an eventual world order where race and nationality will be transcended by international unity. When it is a matter of reform or revolution you are neither the demagogue or the visionary. Yours is the sound, practical approach. In a down-trodden country your first step would not be to hold free elections. You would be more concerned with seeing that everyone had a place to stay and enough food to eat. Your fault may lie in too much moderation. There are times when drastic action is necessary and you are never liable to go to extremes. You do not tend to be affected by your environment. You rely on your own spiritual and mental powers for your well-being. Because you view any problem with such a fair and open mind you are the ideal person to consult for a safe, sane, well-considered judgement. You are aware of every factor and see the heart of the situation. Your ideas may not always seem practical at the time you conceive them; you look so far ahead that in the short term they may not work out as planned. However, you base your conclusions on fundementals and, although accidents may make you appear wrong for a time, in the long run what you predict invariably happens, even though you may not live to see it. Once you have settled on a course of action based firmly on fact you go ahead undaunted by disappointment along the way. You are not influenced by public opinion like the average person. You are an excellent conversationalist; you talk about worthwhile subjects and make pithy, interesting comments. You are intelligent, sensible and well educated. Probably a firm believer in astrology, may even be interested in psychic research. You may also be very musical.

With money you are neither stingy nor profligate; you are always willing to spend for the benefit of others and do not value money for its own sake but rather as a means to an end. Your health is basically sound but you may have obscure nervous disorders. Your habits are temperate, you do not abuse your body. While you are mentally over-active you do not like physical exercise. You are neither too emotional nor too cerebral. You are rational without losing sight of human interests. You are religious though never a bigot, and your sex instinct is well developed, but not to excess, and is in harmony with the rest of your character.

Being a visionary, you have some eccentricities that go along with it. You are a delightful companion, your conversation is stimulating, witty and intelligent. What you have to say is always worthwhile. Because of this any number of people are attracted to you and you choose your friends from every calling and walk of life. While you are very democratic you do not suffer fools gladly. Even with them, however, you understand and therefore forgive.

AQUARIUS AND MARRIAGE

Marriage is not always easy for the Aquarian for you are rarely content to limit yourself to one partner. Your interests are so wide and varied that you require large circles of people to satisfy the many facets of your character. You are therefore more satisfactory to your friends than they are to you, for you contribute something to each of them though it is rare that one of them has as much to offer you.

Nevertheless, you do not make friends in a hurry; once you do, you are extremely loyal. You are not especially subject to physical attractions, your friendships are of the mind and the spirit. You tend to have a wide circle of friends and acquaintances and are especially happy when advising and helping them.

As previously mentioned, it is not always easy for you to settle down with one person. You love all humanity and are prone to becoming interested in a whole series of people. You try first one and then another in an effort to find the ideal. But you have such a fine understanding of human nature that you cannot be deceived by those who do not live up to your high standards. Your love is very idealistic and your mate may be jealous because you have so many friends of the opposite sex. But their fears are without foundation for the most part. Your friends are just that, and you encourage them because of the human interest these associations bring. There is little that is passionate or earthy about you. You are too human for animal instincts to be uppermost. Sometimes you are so idealistic that you transform your love into a love for all mankind and feel obliged to form a mission for the benefit of the world. Undeniably you love your nearest and dearest, but your personal or family ties never prevent you from doing the right thing.

When the time comes, Aquarians make excellent parents; they are very reasonable and understanding but they rarely ever spoil a child. They give their children the freedom to develop as individuals, at the same time guiding them and gently correcting their faults. Some people will tell you that in their experience Aquarians are fine people and people that the world needs. Others that they are eccentric, totally unrealistic and frankly off their heads! Which opinion is formed is dependent upon compatibility. and clearly if the mate forms the latter opinion the marriage will head for the rocks.

AQUARIUS HUSBAND

The Aquarian husband is an idealist, so your relationship with him will depend on how you shape up to his ideals. He can be faithful and sincere in his own way, but this may not be yours. This character cares about everything: the woman who receives a regular bashing from her husband; the stray tom cat down the road who is proud owner of half a tail; the tree outside that looks suspiciously as if it is suffering from Dutch elm disease; pollution, corruption and the whole wide world in general.

If you do not understand him then you can be forgiven for believing that the only thing he does not care about is you. Much depends on your idea of a husband; if it is the solid pillar of society or the pipe and slippers character you require then, with this gent, you have definitely boobed. The Aquarian husband may appear to put the whole world before you but he still cares; it is simply that he knows you are alright.

After all, hasn't he made sure that you have three square meals a day and a roof over your head? But what about the starving millions, or that old tom cat? This man's love may be spread over a wide front but, there is still plenty for you. Come down with beri-beri and you'll see what I mean. However, even his involvement with life is similar to his involvement with love, somewhat detached and intellectual. You will never be able to quite pin him down, but this is why so many women find him attractive. In a crisis you have his undivided attention, but he tells himself that you are a big girl now so therefore you should be able to handle minor problems. Ideally, his woman needs either to share his concern with the world or possess a hundred and one interests of her own. The type of lady who wants to catch him and pin him down simply because she doesn't have enough to occupy her is in for a shock. Not only will he remain elusive but, once he senses demands are being made, he rebels and refuses to co-operate even on the smallest matter. And when an Aquarian can be just as talented at being impossible as the Scorpion or the Taurean. Even though our friend loathes to be unfair he is incapable of occasionally understanding that he is being just that. You'll discover how opinionated he is when listening to him in the throes of so-called "friendly debate". You might think war had been declared. He is quite sure that his viewpoint is the only one worth considering, and you will need a lot of charm or guile, or both, to convince him otherwise. As was initially stated, everything depends on your ability to shape up. "Unfair!" you protest. Maybe, but do leave him alone unless you can accept him as he is. Eccentric, cranky, and a brilliant idiot!

AQUARIUS WIFE

Are you ready for Santa Claus in April? Easter Eggs in December? And your birthday a month later every year? Life may not be quite as crazy as this, but it could be with the Aquarius woman! And why not? She is after all, getting the months right even if she did match them with the wrong occasions. Besides, that way you are growing a month younger every year, so what do you want? Perfection?

Providing you are financially able to pass as a juggler, are heavily involved with your own interests, or better still hers, and are not the over-emotional or highly sexed type, then you are well on your way to being her perfect mate. And do not worry about the strange hours she keeps; chances are it is not a lover she is visiting, but an old lady who lives down the road and has lost her cat. Conversely, she may arrive home exhausted by the spring cleaning she undertook for a sick friend. Yes, you may well be amazed as you sit down among the chaos you call home; but, you see, like her male counterpart, she considers it must suffice that you are both healthy, comfortable and in love. The creatures great and small she worries about have far less in life. The world is her home and you will receive a daily bulletin on its progress.

Didn't you know that the sabre-toothed ... er ... worm, was in danger of extinction? And while you may smile to yourself, remember, it is people like her who are trying to solve the world's problems. We need as many Aquarians as we can lay hands on. Neither is there any point in your thinking that a couple of children will give her something more important to worry about. Yes, she is a good parent, but not a devoted one; it could well be you who will have to surrender leisure time in order to babysit while she runs around performing worthwhile jobs and trying to help the rest of us. Nor will she change with age; she will be as elusive at sixty as she was at sixteen. If you are the kind of sweetly old-fashioned male who thinks of a wife as being warm and cuddly, efficient and motherly, then divorce cannot be far away. But if you enjoy a life full of surprises and can appreciate the value of her outside interests, then step this way. I am sure our friend will be delighted to make your acquaintance.

AQUARIUS AND DIVORCE

The word divorce can hardly be expected to raise one of your eyebrows, never mind strike shock or fear into your heart. It is just as much a part of life as eating or sleeping. So what is all the fuss about? Not surprisingly you'll think nothing of obtaining a decree absolute if it is necessary, assuming, that is, you bothered to marry in the first place, a ceremony which may well have slipped your mind. And also assuming you have noticed your marriage is in trouble, which will not happen unless you are constantly reminded.

So how do you react now that ... er ... whatsisname ... has gone. Oh, you hadn't noticed? Well, take it from me he has! The Aquarian of either sex is enough to send the average solicitor stark, staring bonkers. "What document was that?" you will enquire of him. "No ... I haven't seen it. What did you say your name was?" Crazy conversations like this could delay a divorce for years unless ... er ... whatsisname ... happens to be more together in this direction. But at least there will be no recriminations from our Aquarian friend, no money-grabbing or fights over possessions. The only hitches which do occur in the proceedings will result from the Aquarian's pre-occupation with more important things. Such as ... the fly on the window pane. Will it escape that thumping big spider? Remember, that poor spider has a right to live, a right the Aquarian accepts, and so he/she will watch with abject fascination regardless of the fact that the solicitor went home some time ago! As for the divorce ... better prepare for a long wait.

AQUARIUS EX-HUSBAND

The Aquarian ex can be a pure joy or a weight around the neck, depending upon your point of view. If you are the materialistic type then the latter will apply, for this character has trouble remembering that he has an ex-wife at all, never mind sending off the monthly alimony cheque. Mind you, if you are quite happy to run around and pick it up then maybe life will be easier. One thing is for sure, unless you have six children, you will never see him. At a later date you may find yourself being chatted up by him at a party. You protest. He blushes. He didn't recognize you with your new hairstyle, dress or whatever it is that is different about you, he explains. Tell him you are nine months pregnant and he will not bat an eyelid. He knew there was something different about you, you hear him muttering under his breath as he moved away. Naturally, if you do have shared interests then maybe you will see him occasionally, but don't act surprised if he seems startled when you rise to leave without him. "Where are you going? Oh, yes ... we were divorced, weren't we!"

As an ex-husband the Aquarian isn't that different from the husband, the amount of time you spend with either is about the same. Unless of course you do have those mutual interests!

AQUARIUS EX-WIFE

This is a very similar character to the one above. Therefore she is a positive blessing to the man who would rather not part with his cash or possessions. She will accept what is offered, but will not do battle over material objects. She cannot waste her energy on such trivia. If that ex of hers is a reasonable, responsible individual who regularly sends her a cheque, then they will pile on the dresser until a threatening caller makes it necessary for her to cash one of them. Her erring husband will hardly be surprised when she telephones and thanks him for the present. How sweet of him to send such a nice fat cheque! He will sigh with resignation. After all, isn't this one of the reasons he decided to get rid of this nutcase? Nevertheless, she has her advantages as an ex-wife, once the legalities are over and done with. Despite the fact that he may have tried to shoot, poison or garrotte her all on the same night, this will not prevent her from rushing to his aid if he needs help — providing he telephones, of course. And when he yells for help at four o'clock in the morning, is she annoyed? Not a bit of it! If he is in trouble she will leap to his assistance the same way as she would to any other helpless being. Grudges and the past are all conveniently forgotten. And this is just one of the bonuses of having an Aquarian ex-wife. And it certainly helps when you embark on a remarriage. At least number two will never accuse number one of trying to create trouble, or otherwise introduce discord into the new marriage.

AQUARIUS AND THE COMMUNE

My goodness, you could have a positive field day in this kind of establishment, couldn't you, my Aquarian friend? Imagine the problems you could help solve among the inmates. There would always be someone who could benefit from your humane assistance, and you would invariably dream up ways of improving everyone's lot.

You are a bottomless pit of ideas when it comes to improving the quality of life for others. Yes, the commune would fit the bill nicely, although you would be in danger of entirely sacrificing your own personal life, something you must later regret. Total self-sacrifice belongs to the Piscean, not to you, my friend. Bear this in mind when you move in, and stay for a limited period.

AQUARIUS AND COHABITATION

Your attitude to this state is identical to that of marriage, but this is not surprising when one bears in mind that you are quite capable of forgetting that you had a spouse. However, you may finally wake up when, on reflection, you note that your partner has changed from a fattish redhead in January to a tall blonde in February, to a short brunette in March! Impossible, you will correctly think. Just as well you didn't marry January, isn't it?

Yes ... one thing to be said for this lifestyle is that it will save you endless trips to the divorce courts. An Aquarian may be accused of being amoral, but never immoral. You may have shared your bed with three separate women, but how many did you find time to kiss, never mind make love to? Small wonder you neglected to note the changes that had been going on around you! With your casual approach to relationships and your vague head, it is a wise Aquarian who stays with cohabitation.

AQUARIUS LOVER — MALE

We have already established that the Aquarian is a lover of the world rather than of any one individual. Nevertheless, in spite of this he can, when caught off-guard, become besotted by a member of the opposite sex. Which is reassuring, isn't it? However, the infatuation is short-lived. For two or three glorious weeks he may actually believe that this lady is the incarnation of his ideals and proceed to make her the pivot of his existence. Such an experience can be an unnerving one for her. Suddenly his attention has been switched from the entire universe to focus solely on her. Initially he may wine and dine her, feeling quite sure that this is the thing to do; she may even be lucky enough to extract a bouquet of flowers. If so, she had better make the most of it, they will probably be the last she will ever receive from this character. Once the first week has expired, he brings his spotlight for truth into play. He is beginning to suspect that she is, after all, only mortal. Therefore, he must check up. And he does. But try using the same methods on him and watch him squirm. The second week slips past and all too soon she is revealed in her human frailty. And what is his reaction? Well, he is, of course, now quite satisfied and has once more turned his attention back on the world. Nevertheless, she should not be too dispirited for she has witnessed the nearest he will ever become to being a romantic. If you are the type of lady who insists on her own life and individuality, you have come to the right birth sign, but if your emotional needs are at all time-consuming, or you enjoy an ordered life, then it is suggested that you look elsewhere.

AQUARIUS LOVER — FEMALE

This woman is just about as adept at playing Juliet as her counterpart is to playing Romeo. The rare man may strike oil and enjoy three weeks of her undivided attention, but don't expect any more than this. Furthermore, he will only receive this much adoration if she is totally infatuated by him. But, like her brother Water-Carrier, once she lays bare those human weaknesses she will turn her attention elsewhere. One day, some Aquarian somewhere will dig and scrape away at some lover, only to discover that the paragon is capable of living up to those high ideals. What I wouldn't give to see the Aquarian face then! No man can possibly take on the whole world as a rival, therefore the wisest course for him to steer is to develop as much curiosity as his Aquarian lover. In other words, if you can't beat 'em — join 'em.

AQUARIUS CHILD AND DIVORCE

You mean it has actually been noticed? Then you have produced a possible genius! Obviously if your child is a true blue Aquarian your problems will be minimized, provided you can survive the glare of that spotlight of truth. Insult his or her intelligence and you will quickly be revealed as the fool. Therefore, avoid turning the breakdown of your marriage into a fairy story or a soap opera. Neither is over-simplification the right way to go, especially if your child is a precocious eight or nine-year-old. "Daddy and I don't love each other any more," is not acceptable. "Why?" you will be asked. Avoid at this point attempting to relate how that erring spouse of yours slept with socks on, or worse, with someone else. Try to explain how emotions work, ie., liken love to a plant that needs nourishment, food, light and attention; explain how, in your case, you were both too busy and forgot these things and eventually drifted apart. Your love died so slowly that you hardly noticed. Your Aquarian child will not burst into tears or have nightmares, but will have been taught something valuable and, with any luck, may have learned, when the time comes, to be a little more attentive to his or her own beloved. Once explanations are out of the way, this particular child will return to the business of living quite easily.

Aquarian children will always love both parents in a detached manner, but do not worry about this: it is the only way they know. And do not imagine for one moment that because he or she is living with you, you will be more favoured. The Aquarian is not like the Scorpio or the Taurus child in needing the physical presence of loved ones, and cannot understand those who do. Therefore, be warned — never cling, even if you have no one else in the world. If you try to be constantly possessive and monitor his or her every move you will eventually lose this child.

AQUARIUS CHILD AND REMARRIAGE

Providing your choice of new love is reasonable then you have no problems with this little character. But do remember that you are dealing with an idealist, who may not have you on a pedestal but certainly will have some idea of your true worth as a person. Therefore, if he or she is willing to accept Dracula as his new parent, then I am afraid you are in trouble, for your child's opinion of you is sadly lacking. However, assuming that the young Aquarian's feelings are relatively normal then there will be no need for the new parent to make attempts at measuring up to the departed one, but rather to attempt to be worthy of you. Once the child is convinced this new person is good enough for you, then you will have no further problems. However, it is imperative that you explain to your new love that little Johnny is not the demonstrative type in the hope first of all, that it will be understood that this aloof interest in them can in no way be changed (although this does not mean that there is any lack of devotion). And secondly, it is important that the new parent be aware of the fact that gushing or emotional behaviour is disdained by this child and that is strictly out. Once you have understood and complied with these Aquarian rules, you can then proceed with your new life, confident in the knowledge that your little Aquarian is one hundred per cent in favour of you both.

CONCLUSION

On the previous pages we have looked at the Aquarian's behaviour in various relationships. While it is hoped that this has helped you to avoid certain pitfalls in life, it must be stressed that the final decision, as ever, is with you. Nevertheless, let's sum up. Provided you are a typical Aquarian, then your attitudes and behaviour in marriage and cohabitation will be similar, but as you are temporarily unfit to put up with emotional pressure, you are advised to proceed with caution before tying that knot. You need someone similar to yourself; opposites may attract, but in your case they will not complement. If you are selective enough you have a good chance of finding happiness in marriage.

Cohabitation is a good idea as a testing ground. Otherwise, though you may be quite happy, your frequent absences are going to prove too much of a strain on your partner, and I cannot see the point of your setting up home.

Bachelorhood would save you from the stress you would no doubt have to bear in a close relationship. A night here or there could work out quite well. You do not suffer from loneliness like the other signs; you are too darned busy. You may even be so active that you may never quite get around to consciously settling down, with or without the marriage certificate. Yes, the single state has a lot to offer those born under this sign. Indeed, as does the commune. Your love of humanity really has a chance to shine in these circumstances. Lastly, remember, you are a bit of a loner, so be extra careful when deciding to share your life with anyone. Cast a logical, critical eye over those ideals of yours and you may be able to save yourself a lot of heartaches.

AQUARIUS MARRIAGE CHANCES QUIZ

Answer these questions honestly, and score 3 for yes, 2 for sometimes or unsure, and 1 for no.

1. Do you consciously avoid emotional commitment?
2. Do you believe that marriage is way out of date?
3. Can you think of an alternative to marriage?
4. Are you wary of children?
5. Is the idea of yourself as a doting parent an uncomfortable one?
6. Do you take any active participation in any group connected with helping humanity?
7. Is it difficult for you to remember the last time you stayed in and put your feet up?
8. Is your wardrobe somewhat individual?
9. Do you find possessive behaviour unpalatable?
10. Are you vague? (Ask your mate.)
11. Have you ever been accused of being aloof or cold?
12. Do you take an active part in community affairs?
13. Do you prefer to keep relatives at a safe distance?
14. Would you get up in the middle of the night to help a friend?
15. Are you interested in sport?
16. Does domesticity bore you?
17. Could you survive quite happily on the bearest of necessities?
18. Do you feel unable to cope with emotional outbursts?
19. Do you have a wide circle of friends?
20. Do you need intellectual rapport with a partner more than anything else?

ANSWERS

1 — 30: You may have your sun in Aquarius but you have little else there. Several planets on your personal birth chart must be in Taurus or Scorpio. Read those sections, you could learn a lot about yourself. You are the kind of person who must be married; you may be a strong character but you need another person to give your life meaning and provide a spur for your ambitions. But the rigidity in you makes you a difficult person to live with. Therefore you possess all the qualifications of a deserted husband or wife. Do try to be more flexible.

31 — 50: Yours is the score of the typical Aquarian with more of the virtues of this sign than the vices. You seem to have avoided most of the faults, therefore with a bit of luck you should find that right person and make a happy relationship, married or otherwise. But face up to the fact that it will take time.

51 — 60: Yours is the score of the typical Aquarian with more of the vices of this sign than the virtues. You are a born loner, therefore bachelorhood is your ideal lifestyle. If you have been married before then you will understand just how alien this way of life is to your personality. If you insist on marrying, then expect divorce, as you are an impossible person to live with.

PISCES
(the Fish)
February 20 – March 20

Planet: Neptune
Colour: Sea green
Partners: (In general) Cancer and Scorpio
Countries: Portugal, Normandy, Sudan, Alexandria
Cities: Seville, Bournemouth
Famous Pisceans: Elizabeth Taylor, George Harrison, Rex Harrison, Sidney Poitier, Prince Andrew of England, Victor Hugo, Chopin, John Steinbeck

---

GENERAL CHARACTERISTICS

You are very considerate, sensitive and intuitive. You are so observant, and in so many subtle ways, that you may be considered psychic. In fact, you often are. Your vivid imagination makes you suggestible and impressionable. In negative types this may take the form of illusions and delusions and, in order to preserve them, you may be inclined to over-indulgence in drugs and alcohol. These types are often dreamy and impractical, or detrimentally emotional. There is a tremendous difference between the positive and negative Piscean, the one being able to rise to the top in everything, the other being at the very depths of degradation and despair. The vivid imagination can be abused by the negative types, but it is a source of strength and direction to the positive.

You are so idealistic that you do not appear as practical as you often are. When you have to choose between common sense and theoretical idealism, you use down-to-earth methods. You usually manage to have the material things necessary to your comfort.

If, however, there is a difference between your ideals and the real conditions of your life, you can become restless and discontent and, in order to compensate, can become obsessive about insignificant details.

You are very sympathetic to others but you are usually modest and unassuming, lacking confidence in yourself. You have a very agreeable love nature and are quite domesticated. You are so pleasant that you are quite often the pet of the family. Negative types tend to be lazy and attached to the home, mainly because it is the most comfortable place to be. They have to fight hard for stability and to resist the impulse of the moment. You are very much influenced by your environment and have a tendency to be moulded by it. You are extraordinarily pliable and adaptable. You are not so much concerned with superficial appearances but with inner being. The essence of spirit rather than the concrete physical fact. For you there is little difference between the reality and the dream. You speak and write fluently, are a mystic when it comes to religion and may write about it with divine inspiration.

You are devoted to those you love, sometimes overly so. You are, in fact, self-sacrificing and you do things unselfishly for others and with so little fuss that it may not really be appreciated what you do for them, apparently so effortlessly. And while you do not expect any kind of reward, ingratitude can hurt you deeply. Physically you are not particularly strong and your health, generally, is good. But you have little power to resist disease.

You stretch impressions and create illusions rather than reflect the world as it actually is. You tend to look at life through rose-coloured glasses. You are a dreamer, the idealist who expects the best to happen in this, the best of all possible worlds. You are essentially so romantic that you rarely see life as it really is. You are over-optimistic and can get into trouble through not coming to grips with reality and expecting the best to come out of a wrong situation. You want so much to believe that the world is fine and beautiful, but you must guard against escapism when you find that it is not.

The female Piscean is romantic and feminine and she is tremendously unselfish, trusting and open-handed. Generous to a fault, she gives sympathy and whatever she has to hand to anyone who asks. Others tend to impose upon her as a result. In love she is emotional and voluptuous, but so passive that men all too often take advantage of her. The male Fish is out to attract this type of female. The women in his life will be charming, emotional and will place love above all else. They may not be particularly realistic but their sole aim in life will be to make him happy.

PISCES AND MARRIAGE

You are loving, emotional and idealistic. In personal relationships you are soft and tender, especially when in love. You have an unequalled dedication for passion and self-sacrifice. You are very considerate of others and intuitively know how best to please them. But you do the nice things so quietly and with so little pretence that people all too often fail to appreciate you. In the same way, you love so whole-heartedly and purely and ask so little for yourself in return that those you love tend not to value you as highly as you deserve. You think only of giving pleasure to your loved ones; that is very often where you give yourself completely. You are truly devoted once you have given your love. On the other hand, you are not especially particular about the kind of person you give your heart to. You may feel that there is great nobility in loving someone inferior, who depends on you and solely needs your love. In fact, the tendency is not to use your head at all but rather depend upon intuition where your affections are concerned. You are charming, romantic and poetic, there is a great delicacy in your love's expression.

Because of the above characteristics certain dangers exist for the Piscean in marriage. You must be careful in your approach to emotional relationships for you tend to get carried away and discover too late that the marvellous attributes you saw do not really exist. You will find it difficult to cope with the practical aspects of marriage. You make a wonderful lover and have a real flair for the romantic. But when it comes to handling those bills or that nasty green stuff, let's face it, you're hopeless.

As parents, Pisceans find it difficult to insist on any form of correction, even verbal. There is, for that reason, a strong tendency for their children to be spoilt. Although Piscean parents will give their children a splendid artistic background, you must recognize your failings in practical matters — tidiness, punctuality and so on. And make certain that your children do not copy you, as they often learn from example; it may be left to your partner to solve this problem. Because of your sensitivity, my dear Piscean friend, you need to use that head a little more if you are to avoid making a mistake.

PISCES HUSBAND

Have you as much romance in your soul as Elizabeth Browning, the patience of a saint and the ability to care of Florence Nightingale? Yes? Then you are the ideal lady for the Piscean husband. But if you are as independent as Germaine Greer, as power-crazed as Cleopatra, or as promiscuous as Nell Gwynn then you are in for a hard time if you want this man in your life. Our friend is a paradox. He expects his woman to be open with him, and yet he has a distinct secret side to his personality. He is complexity himself, for although he insists that she understand him, he will resent it when she does; nevertheless, he isn't a bad proposition for the right female. But she needs to be unconcerned or unimpressed with worldly success or possessions. The Piscean is not that ambitious. He wishes to be free to grow and develop without pressure, this is why many well-known members of this sign are poets, artists and writers. When success does arrive, it is rarely through his own doing, more an accident of fate. Not that he isn't talented enough to deserve it, but he does need someone to manage him, someone who can attract attention to him. He certainly will not. Neither is he impressed by his admirers. He wants to be alone to create. When the Piscean has to work out of necessity in a factory or an office, then he is sure to have an artistic hobby. And he should be encouraged in expressing this part of his personality. Apart from being free of worldly cares, his lady must also be a romantic; he is the type who always sends flowers or writes poetry or both. He does not take her love for granted. He wonders at it. How can she love such a worthless fool as he? Yes, he is also modest. She must be prepared for a house full of weird and wonderful things, strange animals, plus several children.

Therefore, career ladies are just not suitable. He is gentle and spiritual; he is also indecisive, financially hopeless and infuriatingly impractical. But if you are content to be his wife, a mother to him and the children, also his lover and financial wizard, then you could be in for a life in which love and peaceful co-existence are paramount. Many women believe that this gentleness and weakness can be knocked out of him, and he can be made to shape up with them. Rubbish! Heaven help them, for are they in for a shock! Our friend will not change, and when you try to make him, like the fish he swims this way then that, if he can avoid your influence. And if you persist, one day he will literally slip through your fingers for good. Just like the silvery Fish he is.

PISCES WIFE

The Piscean wife is perhaps easier to handle than her male counterpart, mainly because many men expect a woman to be hopeless with money and to be content to stay at home with the housework and family. They are, of course, misinformed gentlemen, but this is not a book on equality, so I will refrain from further comment! Nevertheless, this is the kind of man Mrs Pisces needs. The typical Piscean lady is not a careerist. If she works, it is for practical reasons, not out of a desire for fame and fortune. She is defenceless in the face of pressure in any form, and needs a strong man to lean on. I am not talking about physical attributes; he can be a runt of a man but one that is prepared to take all the responsibilities and be totally devoted. This devotion must be expressed regularly and romantically. Any man who fits the bill will gain plenty in return.

The Piscean wife is a hundred per cent female and she lives and breathes only for her man. Her hypersensitivity is a characteristic that helps her to sense and cater to his lightest whim. She invariably makes the most of her physical appearance and always appears delightfully, femininely well groomed. Even the mousiest Fish can exhibit the sexiest of vibrations and can cleverly transform her ordinary face into something worth a second look, not only with paint and powder but also with expression. When she is in love she positively glows, but take her love away and you'll wonder why you ever thought her attractive. So you can imagine how outstandingly attractive the really beautiful Fish can be. Elizabeth Taylor is a good example. This lady has appeared to be an unbeatable beauty in her time, but when her love life has gone wrong the face dulls and, my, don't those inches gather! But to return to our subject. As a parent the Piscean wife is the most loving of all. In fact, because she gives and gives and gives, to both husband and children, she should always be on her guard against overdoing it, for in some cases she may give until there is nothing left for herself.

Pisces is the sign of self-sacrifice. Because of this it is all too easy to take advantage of her, but it is most unkind to do so. The Piscean lady has her faults, but as a wife she is unsurpassable.

PISCES AND DIVORCE

Divorce can be a destructive exercise for the true Fish. Naturally, if it is the Piscean who has lost the matrimonial home then life will be easier. But one can be sure that this character would not desert the family residence unless a new love was tucked away somewhere. In these circumstances the Fish can survive the experience admirably with the help of the new love. There will, of course, be times when painful moods stimulated by guilt are experienced but these will become less as time passes.

However, what about the deserted Fish? They find it difficult to cry, "Yippee, freedom!" Their broken hearts and life take time to heal and rebuild. Nevertheless, the Piscean will not fight proceedings; if this is what the erring spouse needs, then OK, an unwilling partner is no use to the Fish. The Piscean will sign all necessary papers, though they will be returned tearstained, and do whatever is required. Pisceans may feel desperate or unable to continue living, but do not become embittered or revengeful. These individuals have no desire to hurt the once-adored mate, and it is not easy to abandon a member of this sign. One thing is certain, the erring spouse will never again be the subject of such worship. Not unless they manage to locate another Piscean. Later, indeed, this fact may hit home with full force, and when it does the departed lover may make several attempts at reconciliation. All well and good if the first one is successful; if not the whole ghastly experience will begin again. Hopefully the Piscean will never be deserted unless the spouse is absolutely sure they do not wish to return. There are, of course, those who will take advantage of the Fish's good nature. They are for ever popping backwards and forwards to the matrimonial home. In this instance the only hope for the Fish lies in the strength of the eventual new love. For, make no mistake, this Fish is rarely alone for long. Number two may have the unhappy tasks of chasing away number one before all can settle down and enjoy.

PISCES EX-HUSBAND

The identity of the guilty party is unimportant to this character. All that counts is that love has flown out of the window. Incriminations are not a talent of his and this is reflected in his attitude to alimony. He tends to be generous but erratic. Remember he was never any good at sorting out the finances when he was married and this hasn't changed at all. The unscrupulous female would have no difficulty in bleeding the poor man white, unless he has found a new strong love who is exercising some influence over him. Without a mate this man is particularly vulnerable and he certainly needs a good solicitor really devoted to protecting his welfare.

Assuming then that finances have been satisfactorily sorted out, what kind of ex-husband are you? Not a wise one, I'm afraid. You allow yourself to worry and fret about your ex, long after the decree nisi has been granted. You often appear to become an emotional doormat when what you should be doing is worrying about yourself. Besides, consider for a moment that this kind of behaviour is going to make things very tough on your new lady when she eventually turns up. She will not be enamoured by tales of your ex's problems, or obligations you feel towards this party. Oh, no ... you may not be considering this possibility now, but, believe me, it will not be long before it is a reality. You rarely chase the opposite sex; they quite often pursue you, sometimes quite relentlessly. So get yourself back into physical shape. Hire an asbestos vest for that vulnerable heart and start living once more. Join a club that will get you out into the big wide world again. Despite the fact that you are hiding at home and not attending a million parties, why not make a personal vow: for every four invitations you receive, accept one. The main thing is for you to pick yourself up as quickly as possible before your reclusive tendencies take over. Bacherlorhood has its compensations if you look for them. Regard it as a temporary condition.

PISCES EX-WIFE

Regardless of your status, any Piscean lady on her own is lonely. Because of your soft heart you can fall even deeper into the identical trap that awaits your brother Fish. "He's not earning enough money to pay my alimony," or "He has so many problems, I must help!" are statements that should be stricken from your vocabulary. Naturally, if you are financially independent that's good, but if not, you must be practical. As for his problems, I'm sure that you have enough of your own to keep you occupied. You have a duty to yourself now, so no matter how depressed you are feeling, lover number two is not that far away. In these days of womens liberation your value as a traditional female has shot up out of all proportion, for if the role of women is slowly changing, at present men are pretty much the same. Many of them want a devoted lady who is happy to revolve her life around them, and aren't these your specialities? Your feminity brings out the protector in practically every man you meet, but the key word here is "meet". You are not going to help yourself by sitting at home every night, are you? Charity or social work may be the answer temporarily if you must worry about someone else, and later, when you feel ready, start accepting those invitations. Surely you don't believe that, with all the men in the world, your ex was the epitome of manhood? After all, if he were then you are unlikely to have allowed him to slip through your fingers. Not with your intuition. Face up to the fact that your marriage is dead and let it lie down. There is a new life waiting for you. Isn't it about time you got your fingers on it?

PISCES AND THE COMMUNE
In the right circumstances the commune could work for you but you would need to enter this establishment with a partner. You may be good at sacrificing yourself but this could only work for a limited period without that special someone by your side. Conversely, with a partner you could both cheerfully rush around attempting to make life comfortable and happy for a bevy of people. And, who knows, you may be blissfully happy. But personally I believe that this situation could be tantamount to allowing several people to use you as a doormat. Regrettably this is human nature, the sooner someone seems to be prepared to take on our worries and problems, we tend to sit back and allow them to do it. In time we even expect it. Therefore, although this lifestyle may make you happy for a while, when you later realize that you have become the communal emotional dumping-ground then even you must raise objections, despite the fact that it could take years for you to reach this decision. Far better that your devotion be given to a smaller group of people, otherwise you may wear yourself out.

PISCES AND COHABITATION
The Piscean is too sensitive and insecure to take on this life-style unless it is to be a trial marriage. A relationship without commitment is not for you. When you make commitments you like to make them to the fullest extent. The "I dig you, baby — let's shack up together for a while!" is simply not on in your book. You cannot syphon out the correct amount of love to fit the occasion. It is all or nothing, and all means courtship, marriage and eventually a family. Practical considerations are not sufficient reason for you to live with a member of the opposite sex, therefore do not allow yourself to be swayed by the "Everybody's doing it" argument. Everybody is not you; and, besides, ask yourself if everybody is happy? "Do your own thing" is much more appropriate for the Piscean.

PISCES LOVER — MALE
A tag you will happily don anytime! As long as it is applicable. In view of the above section, it is to be assumed that you are in the throes of a trial marriage, a state of affairs that will not last long. For as soon

as your lady realizes what a treasure she has, she will march you down the aisle at the first opportunity. That is, unless your judgement is at fault, which is rarely the case, for you are usually protected by your splendid intuition. As a lover you are sweetly old-fashioned. Some of the most beautiful poetry was written by Pisceans in love. You court your love in every sense of the word. Compliments, presents and a natural talent for saying the right thing at the right time usually guarantee your success. Sexually speaking you are also quite a catch. Stealthy groping or a direct assault on your victim is not your style. You rely almost exclusively on emotional spontaneity. However, you do not take too kindly to a refusal when you are bursting with love. But then what female in her right mind could deny you in such circumstances? Neither do you expect your lady to slave away in the house, or cooking for you; if she does you are overwhelmed, but you are not the type who runs his fingers along the tops of bookcases in an effort to make a point. All you need is love, everything else you receive you regard as a bonus. Nevertheless, you have one big drawback — enormous, in fact, to certain females. You are pretty hopeless when it comes to finance. Therefore let's hope your Juliet has a practical head on her shoulders. Otherwise you may find your love nest violated by the bailiffs, and there will be no point in your lover expecting you to come up with helpful suggestions – you will probably have disappeared. Or, at the very least, stuck your head in the wall-to-wall carpeting! However, providing your lover is prepared to put up with this then she will have little other reason for complaint.

PISCES LOVER — FEMALE

This is the lover for you if you like a woman who can make you feel like Paul Newman and Paul Getty all rolled into one — and what man doesn't? Hence the Pisces lady is very much in demand. This female, and I mean *female*, will greet you when you arrive home from work wearing some silky, satiny or fluffy creation which will make you want to devour her on sight. A delicious smell will be wafting from the kitchen and your favourite beverage will be awaiting your attention. Bliss, you think, so filled with anticipation you sink into your favourite chair. Suddenly something catches your eye. "What are these?" you enquire waving in the general direction of a pile of envelopes. She sweetly smiles, "Nothing," she insists, "just a pile of nasty bills I have been collecting over the last few months and have been meaning to give you." Suddenly everything goes black. You rush into the kitchen in order to locate some candles, where you turn on the gas stove for some light ... nothing. Finally you find the wax objects and affix one to a saucer. "It must be a fuse," you mutter on your way to the telephone, "I'll ring old Frank next door. Such a practical chap!" You pick up the receiver. Silence. Then you remember the ominous pile of letters ... Everything suddenly becomes abundantly clear. Nothing has been paid. All the bills are there, together with your bank statement. All are, of course, equally as threatening, all promising legal proceedings, unless etc., etc.

But hold it right there. Did you really expect that loving bundle of yours to sort out such unpleasant things? No, I am afraid, my friend, that if you are determined to spend your life with a Piscean wife then it must be you who attends to such mundane things. With any luck you have a sense of humour, for when she realizes that the least she could have done is draw your attention to the bills, she will take full responsibility for your present state and will cry buckets. What do you do? Kiss away the tears and have an early night is my suggestion. Not much else you can do without light, heat etc., However, isn't the love you are enjoying worth just a little aggravation? Of course it is!

PISCES CHILD AND DIVORCE

Whether your Piscean child is two or twelve, the consequences of divorce are not going to be easy, and you may as well accept it. That little Fish is so dependent upon his or her parents, that it is going to take a long time, a lot of love and reassurance before you convince this child that it hasn't been abandoned or rejected. The reasons for your marriage breakdown are of no interest; all that counts is the end product: a lost parent. You'll need to make an appeal to the Piscean child's emotions. "We don't love each other any more," is easily understood, although the young Fish's first thought will be what will happen if you suddenly don't love him any more? Will he be placed in an orphanage? You will have to explain the different types of love that exist, stressing again and again that the love a parent has for a child is indestructible. He will be placated if you can get this point across. It may take weeks and months of constant reassurance, but such patience is required if your Fish is to grow into a normal adult, whatever that may mean.

If the young Piscean becomes over-emotional in the ensuing months, don't worry; this is a good sign. The danger arises should he insist on hiding in his room for hours on end dry-eyed, for this is a very unhappy Fish. You must then do all you can to draw the child out. Hysteria, reproaches and floods and floods of tears are all eminently preferable and natural; indifference is a bad sign with this little character. Remember, a dry Fish is a dead one. Try to keep that in mind and it will help you considerably. When he realizes that he will be seeing the missing parent quite regularly he will begin to relax. But this will not be until the new routine has been firmly established, and this is going to take time. So do not expect him to feel secure immediately. Once he does, however, recovery can only be just around the corner.

PISCES CHILD AND REMARRIAGE

Remarriage of the beloved parent is easier for the Fish to accept than the divorce, for the feelings will be of gaining and not being deprived. Naturally, to achieve this happy state the child will need reassurance from you that your love is big enough for two, and this is something you will need to prove with actions; words alone are insufficient. After all, you have already explained about the different types of love, so the love you are giving to someone else won't be taken from the love you feel for your child. It will be easier if the new parent is a member of the opposite sex to the child, but a new parent will need to tread carefully for several months before they are accepted. Discipline, for example, will not be tolerated from an outsider. Only when a newcomer feels that he/she is completely accepted can they start laying down the law. In the meantime all discipline must come from the real parent. It will be obvious when the new parent has been accepted, for when a Fish loves he or she cannot help but show it. The first time the new parent is allowed to kiss away the tears when the child grazes a knee, or becomes desperate because maths homework is too hard, either or both of these will be signs of acceptance. Try to buy this child's love and you are in for a disappointment. No matter how expensive the gift, he or she will politely thank you and put it away in the toy cupboard. One day you will make a plane or something out of pieces of scrap, or will knit a sweater for the favourite Teddy bear and the child's arms will be thrown around your neck — yet another Piscean way of saying "I love you". Once you have achieved this, you have the responsibility never to break that trusting little heart. Now that you are accepted you are free to punish him when he is naughty or kiss him when he is good. When you first smack his bottom he will cry, naturally, but it won't be long before the sun shines out of his face again. Always look for the emotion; even hatred is better than indifference, in this instance anyway. Besides, the very fact that you can make his real Daddy or Mummy laugh or feel happy is reason enough for him to love you. Pisces and remarriage can prove to be very compatible, with help and lots of love.

CONCLUSION

It doesn't take an Einstein to work out that marriage is by far the most desirable state for members of this sign. Cohabitation is fine if marriage is to be the end result, but not as a permanent state. Bachelorhood is too lonely and the commune too self-destructive. Most Pisceans are given the natural ability to make others happy, therefore all you need is the right partner. So be discriminating. Divorce is an unpleasant experience unless you have a new love waiting in the wings. Emotionally you are romantic, conventional and old-fashioned. Do not allow yourself to be influenced by other people. Follow the dictates of your own heart and you will survive splendidly. You may fantasize about being Don Juan or Modesty Blaise, but it will never amount to anything in reality. This is just not your scene. In truth the world has enough swingers and most of them are unhappy. We could do with a few more souls like you, so please don't make excuses for yourself or your way of life. You know what makes you happy, right? Right.

PISCES MARRIAGE CHANCES QUIZ

Answer these questions honestly and score 3 for yes, 2 for sometimes or unsure, and 1 for no.

1. Are you a romantic?
2. Is financial wizardry above you?
3. Do you have an artistic job or hobby?
4. Are you indecisive?
5. Do you prefer to stay away from the rat-race of success?
6. Are you sensitive?
7. Do you love animals?
8. Are your family and partner all that are important to you?
9. Are you bewildered in a financial crisis? (Ask your mate.)
10. Are you secretly relieved when passed over for promotion?
11. Do you write poetry or verse?
12. Have you a secretive side?
13. Are you emotional?
14. Do you doubt your ability to survive in this big world alone?
15. Do you dislike your own company?
16. Do you get a secret kick out of self-sacrifice? (Be honest.)
17. Does violence on TV or films sicken you?
18. Do you ignore problems until you feel able to cope?
19. Do you believe in marriage.
20. Do you find that the countryside has a relaxing effect on you?

ANSWERS

1 — 30: Your Sun may be in Pisces but other planets on your birth chart must be in more practical signs. Try reading the sections on Virgo or Capricorn: you could learn quite a lot about yourself. Your marriage chances are fairly good but you allow yourself to be diverted by a preoccupation with ambition and money. This could have a damaging effect on your relationship and you need to learn more about your own emotions and those of your mate.

31 — 50: This is the score of the Piscean in possession of more of the better qualities associated with this sign. You are a joy to know and love. You certainly deserve a happy marriage. Be discriminating and you will achieve one.

51 — 60: This is the score of the Fish who possesses too many of the Piscean faults. You lean too heavily on those you love, drawing their time and energy like an emotional vampire. Because of this you are placing yourself in a precarious position, and not too many people can live under such a strain. You could well be an excellent candidate for deserted husband or wife of the year, and maybe not just once.

HOW PERFECT IS YOUR RELATIONSHIP?

When a marriage or lengthy relationship breaks down there can, of course, be many reasons. Alcoholism, the pretty blonde down the road, financial problems, deception in its many guises, etc. The list is apparently endless. But wait a minute, all of these are, basically the end product or the result of something which was lacking in the relationship in the first place. There are two far greater enemies to a relationship than any of the above: lack of communication and guilt. Both can nibble away at two people and their love until one day there is nothing left. Or of course they may remain buried, in which case there are various avenues of escape open to the persons concerned. Namely those listed above. In an effort to discover whether your relationship is beginning to show symptoms of distress — read on.

COMMUNICATION:

Saying the hardest things is like making love. It gets easier and better with practice. Telling your husband or lover that you would like to make love on the sitting-room floor instead of always in the bedroom will not necessarily break your relationship, and once you have said it and you see for yourself that it hasn't done any damage; you'll find you are not as anxious the next time you have something difficult to say. Would you dare say the following:

1. I know you want to make love now but I am really not in the mood.
2. There is something you do that really annoys me.
3. You don't always sexually satisfy me.
4. You don't always fulfil my needs.
5. Please leave me alone; I want to think.
6. Can't we try something sexually different?
7. You are putting on weight.
8. We are not as close as we used to be.
9. I feel bored and restless.
10. I thought Jack/Jill was sexually very attractive.

With these statements there are several fears involved. We basically don't want to hurt our lover, we don't want to lose their respect or love, and lastly we are frightened that we will make ourselves too vulnerable. Obviously one should not confront a lover with more honesty than they can absorb at one time; that is just asking for trouble. The best thing to do is to find the least hurtful thing you wish to discuss, prefix your statement with, "I do love you, darling, but ..." and plunge in. Once the complaint has been brought out into the open, it can then be discussed and communication has been established. A word of warning, however; this is a two-way street, for your partner may be equally wary of confessing some dissatisfaction with you. Even if the whole procedure does end in a row, this is infinitely preferable to burying your complaints in the hope that they will go away. They won't; besides, kissing and making up can be tremendous fun!

GUILT:

To find out possible sources of guilt, which can also inhibit communication, answer the following questions:

1. Have you ever been physically attracted to someone else while your lover has been present?
2. Is there any sexual pleasure you have enjoyed in the past that you have not enjoyed with your present lover?
3. Have you ever been with your lover when you would much rather have been alone?
4. Have you ever pretended to enjoy sex with your lover?
5. Do you like his/her friends or relatives?
6. Are there any of his/her friends or relatives you particularly dislike?
7. Do you feel the amount of sexual relations you enjoy with your lover is too much, too little, or just right?
8. Does he/she have habits or characteristics that annoy you?
9. Have you had to make a career change for practical reasons that would not have been necessary had you not met him/her?
10. Does your lover understand your work and its problems?

Once you know which specific areas of your relationship inspire the most guilt or fear, you are also aware of what you most need to discuss. The two generally tend to go together very neatly.

Many of the things you find difficult to communicate are connected with sex. Here, timing is all-important. If you are going to start criticizing technique in the middle of love-making then you must have a death wish! Conversely, using the good feeling and pleasant relaxation that follows love-making is excellent timing. In a close relationship the bedroom is usually the best place to discuss most problems, but in certain cases, boudoir is often a battleground. We assume, sometimes incorrectly, that merely being together in bed constitutes intimacy. Psychiatrists will tell us that physical intimacy often isn't intimacy at all but an effort to avoid it. But, of course, if your relationship is at this stage then it may take more than a few talks to resolve your problems. Generally speaking, in a love relationship the bedroom may be the best place to have your serious discussions. Again check that timing; before or during love aren't examples of common sense. Neither is demanding your partner hear a revelation while he/she is almost asleep.

Making some kind of physical contact with your partner can create a better mood for the sharing of important feelings. Eye contact also helps, although it may not be that easy for you. In general, if there is enough love, caring and communication, then no problem is too big to drive you apart. And if you have a good relationship, hang on to it and be prepared to put some effort into it. Emotions are like plants; without water they wither and die. If you always bear this in mind then your chances of success will be greatly increased.

HOW INDEPENDENT ARE YOU?

Are you always yourself, no matter what? Or do you change? Or can you run with the hare and the hounds in an effort to conform to the attitudes of your friends, relatives, family, neighbours, lovers? This quiz explores your personality and its areas of freedom and dependency. Answer the questions honestly, for some of them are more difficult than they seem. When you have done the quiz you will be able to discover your level of independence. Score as explained and then turn to page 147 for the answers:

1. At a party you meet a man/woman who really attracts you and you can tell they are interested too. A friend then takes you aside and says, "Let me tell you: he/she is bad news. Run like hell!" Now do you:
   (a) run as suggested; you have had enough trouble in your short life?
   (b) nod your head in thanks but prefer to make your own judgement?
   (c) ignore the advice; you like her/him and the warnings are probably exaggerated anyway?
2. You are a strong believer in capitalism, stronger punishment for criminals and the abolition of the welfare system, but many of your friends are liberals. When they tell you their views, do you:
   (a) argue strenuously for your beliefs?
   (b) change the subject?
   (c) indicate quietly and unargumentatively that you don't agree?
   (d) say nothing?

3. You've been comfortably entrenched in a relationship for several years and the person you are fond of is OK but doesn't really sweep you off your feet. Suddenly just like in a fairy story, you fall crazily in love with someone else and they with you. Do you:
   (a) have a quiet, discreet affair?
   (b) ask for a divorce or break the relationship?
   (c) say a woeful goodbye to your new love because you couldn't bring yourself to face all the dramas?

4. The company you work for is going out of business. Several courses of action are open to you. Would you:
   (a) apply for a job like your old one?
   (b) move to a new better paid job for which you have to assume more responsibility?
   (c) take a chance on going into business on your own with hopes of achieving profits and independence should you succeed?

5. When hotly pursued by two or three members of the opposite sex, would you:
   (a) have affairs with them all?
   (b) go out with them but not commit yourself physically until you have singled out one you liked the best?
   (c) pick the most attractive and have an affair with him or her first?

6. How do you choose your new clothes? By:
   (a) browsing or window-shopping until you find what you want?
   (b) reading through magazines to see what's new?
   (c) taking someone with you who knows what is in fashion?

7. Your new lover is attractive and adores you, but seems unable to satisfy you sexually. Would you:
   (a) be patient, believing that sexual rapport will come?
   (b) straightforwardly ask him or her to do things that bring you satisfaction?
   (c) show him or her what to do to please you?

8. Your lover has a setback in his/her career and must go through six months or more of unemployment. Would you:
   (a) support him or her uncomplainingly?
   (b) suggest a separation until he or she is solvent again?
   (c) support him or her but insist that they take over the household chores, and have dinner ready for you when you come home?

9. When criticized do you react with:
   (a) anger; nobody is going to undermine you?
   (b) interest, for you like to know how other people see you and might be able to improve yourself?
   (c) discomfort, for you hate to be found wanting?
   (d) indifference, for you know you are right and the negative

opinion of you is immaterial?

10. If you were the head of your country, would you want to:
    (a) be involved, controversial and public-spirited?
    (b) be a true father or mother figure but one who would take advice from others?
    (c) do things your way and to hell with everybody else?
    (d) be very active in the areas you understand and ignore the others?

11. You are going to a function where you are likely to get a lot of publicity. Would you:
    (a) wear something which compliments your best physical attractions?
    (b) your standard best outfit, you don't care much about clothes?
    (c) wear something outrageous, you do like to attract attention?
    (d) something quiet and elegant?

12. How do you feel about falling in love with someone who has several obvious faults and drawbacks:
    (a) You'd accept the fact that they aren't perfect and hope to help them.
    (b) Although you care, these defects would embarrass you and eat away at the respect you feel.
    (c) If you loved them you would love the whole person, spots, dandruff and all.
    (d) Impossible, you could never care deeply enough for someone with any serious faults.

13. You have just won a competition and you are offered the choice of four locations to visit, expenses paid, would you go on:
    (a) an African safari?
    (b) a cruise to the South Sea Islands?
    (c) a deluxe tour of Europe?
    (d) a journey to some really remote place such as Afghanistan or Tibet?

14. Somehow, perhaps because he or she is a member of your family, you have an important movie star to stay with you. Would you:
    (a) arrange a party to show him or her off and invite everybody?
    (b) try to seduce him/her?
    (c) be somewhat intimidated and arrange to have a good friend to lend moral support?
    (d) keep hangers-on away, but otherwise treat him or her like any other guest?

SCORING:

Question 1 — A2, B6, C10

Question 2 — A10, B4, C6, D2

Question 3 — A6, B8, C2

Question 4 — A2, B6, C10

Question 8 — A2, B8, C10

Question 9 — A10, B6, C2, D8

Question 10 — A10, B2, C6, D6

Question 11 — A4, B10, C6, D2

Question 5 — A8, B2, C4   Question 12 — A4, B2, C6, D10
Question 6 — A10, B6, C4   Question 13 — A6, B4, C2, D10
Question 7 — A2, B10, C4   Question 14 — A4, B8, C2, D10

100 — 136: To others, your single-minded pursuit of your goals may
seem somewhat ruthless but you are not really unkind, in fact, you are
quite a loyal friend. As a person who takes their own risks you don't
like being told what to do and are apt to resent the friendliest of
advice. You are something of an adventurer, may even at times flirt
with danger, and when your life gets too dull you are quite openly
bored. The only person for you is someone equally strong and
independent. Unfortunately you tend to attract the weaker types. If
you are a woman you are certainly liberated and perhaps a little too
much so. But, for both sexes, in your search for independence you
tend to cut yourself off from free and easy interchange with those
around you.

74 — 98: Ever thought of going into politics? People are attracted to
your warm, open personality. Diplomacy, however, doesn't come
easily, and you often hurt the feelings of close friends and lovers
without intention. Relationships with the opposite sex are apt to be
stormy since some of them resent your competitiveness and blithe
habit of going your own way without discussing what should be done
with them. You could have earned the highest score on the
independence scale.

44 — 72: You are a usually well-balanced and happy person, but
tend to be affected by sudden self-doubt and lack of confidence
whenever you try to steer a course too far away from the opinions of
your friends and relatives. But as long as you feel loved and accepted
without your group, you feel quite free to be open, forthright and even
dissident. But you are easily hurt by hostility or criticism. You are
certainly brought down by an unhappy love affair and can nurse your
wounds for days, weeks, even months before cheering up. But then
here is the bright side: as you grow more mature you will gain extra
confidence and begin to earn your own self-approval.

28 — 42: You are a person who needs others. You make sure there
are always plenty of people around. Your life is a network of
interdependencies, favours owed and received, shared meals, shared
lovers, shared everything. You feel quite friendly usually, so what is
the point in trying to develop a harsh individualistic point of view?
You find happiness without it.

YOUR CHANCES OF DIVORCE

Astrologically speaking, certain birth signs possess a greater chance of achieving success within marriage than others. There is no evil star which prevents any member of this or that sign from being happy, it is simply that there are some characteristics which are not compatible with lengthy relationships and these characteristics can usually be located under a particular Zodiac sign. Listed below are all twelve signs. The one at the top, Cancer, indicates that subjects born under this sign have the greatest chance of finding happiness within marriage, and so on down the line. Check out your partner. Is that man or woman of yours really as domesticated as they appear? Or maybe you are the type who prefers a change of partner every few years!

CANCER June 22 — July 22
Cancerians occupy the top of the list due to their natural domesticity and need for a family. This individual is also a sensitive soul, in many cases to the extreme. Nevertheless, marriage offers an attractive protection for this type. So tenacious are members of this sign that they are unlikely to let go once a partner has been chosen. Because of this, while the chances of a long-lasting relationship are good, in many instances this does not necessarily make for happiness with such a clinging attitude, which can at times be overbearing. Providing it is possible to be tolerant regarding this particular trait, then marriage can work out well, for this is a natural home-maker and one who enjoys giving love to others.

TAURUS April 21 — May 21
The Taurean knows exactly what he/she wants, and this equally applies where marriage is concerned. Once this type has picked a mate, fidelity follows easily. This character needs a safe and solid background if he/she is to succeed professionally. The Taurean becomes lazy and apathetic when alone, but with another person to fight for, this character's splendid determination surfaces. The stubbornness which accompanies this sign is certainly valuable in times of want or stress. Beware, however, for the same characteristic will lead Taureans into sticking around even if they are miserable, for they loathe admitting defeat. Possessiveness is yet a further trait given

to those under this sign. And claustrophobia is a common complaint associated with their loved ones.

CAPRICORN December 22 — January 20

Although flirtatious, the Capricorn will rarely stray. The male is an ambitious creature; he calculates his path through life and works towards professional success. His counterpart, too, aims for this, and she is most unlikely to be lured into bed just for the sake of it. She pushes her husband and children up the ladder of success, and while the husband is climbing he is hardly likely to be deterred by a pretty face. However, such single-mindedness can on occasion stimulate feelings of neglect in their partners, although the Capricorn will probably be too busy even to notice.

SCORPIO October 24 — November 22

Scorpions are neither easy to catch nor to dispose of. But at least they can be extremely loyal, providing that you fit in with their ideals and ideas. They do not like to be thwarted, for they hate failure of any description. They may not even realize they are unhappily married until it is brought to their notice by a third party. If they are lucky enough to find the right mate, however, they possess one problem – or virtue, depending upon your point of view — for this character is very highly sexed. Therefore, problems may arise if the partner's appetites are not quite so keen.

VIRGO August 24 — September 23

Virgoans have a relatively good chance of making a successful marriage, simply because they rarely commit themselves until totally convinced that the party concerned is able to live up to expectations. Besides, they need someone to think about apart from themselves. Virgoans are hard workers and they need an objective. Furthermore, they enjoy devoting themselves to others. However, when disappointed with the partner, the Virgoan, although not rushing into the divorce court, tends to make life somewhat unbearable with a constant stream of criticisms and complaints.

AQUARIUS January 21 — February 19

This is the sign of the idealist. Aquarians take their time about choosing a life partner. When suitably mated they have no desire to make life complicated by chasing a bit of fun on the side. Generally speaking, they are far too busy sorting out the world and its problems: for them this introduces quite enough complexity into their lives. Here again, however, such an active life can lead to feelings of neglect in loved ones and, should the partner taken it further and wander away for a while, the Aquarian will not be thrown off-balance. Where members of this sign commit themselves they NEVER make a mistake! All Aquarians know that. They prefer to live with it, rather than admit such fallibility.

THE FOLLOWING SIGNS ARE THOSE PRONE TO MULTIPLE MARRIAGES:

LEO July 23 — August 23

Leonines find life alone impossible, for they are warm, generous and hypersensitive. Because of their fondness for company they are too prone to rush into marriage without taking time to consider what they are doing. They fall in love totally with some imaginary person and are greatly perturbed when Mr and Miss Ideal turn out to be human or worse! Lions are notoriously bad judges of character and too inclined to marry anyone who can boost their ever-flagging egos; but it is difficult not to love a Leo, if only for a while.

PISCES February 20 — March 20

Pisceans need to be married, never mind to whom, just as long as they are within this happy state. This is the weakest and most gentle of all the signs but Pisceans do need a special person as a mate, and this person is apparently difficult to find. Women believe the male of this species to be irresponsible and sensitive and are inclined to dismiss him as being too weak, which obviously results in a lack of respect. Conversely, men find the female Piscean too unworldly, clinging and dreamy. But both the sexes are attractive and kind people, so while they have no difficulty in finding a mate, it is often the wrong one. Those born under this sign should look for a partner who is understanding and as sensitive as they are. A modicum of common sense should also be present, or financial problems will be prominent within the relationship.

LIBRA September 24 — October 23

Librans constantly search for pleasure and perfect love. This leads to a continual stream of new partners. Love, to them, must always be on a grand romantic scale. This is a little wearing for the rest of us, especially the more practical who realize that one cannot live with one's feet permanently off the ground. It is not impossible for the Libran to find happiness within marriage, if the partner is happy to revolve his/her world around them. At least this type has plenty to offer, but beware, for they will expect twice as much in return. So many demands can kill the romance in a relationship, although the Libran is unlikely to recognize the fact.

GEMINI May 22 — June 21

Geminians need to be married, although they rarely admit it. Those born under this sign are cerebral creatures whose minds seek constant nourishment. Therefore, they chase challenge and stimulation at the drop of a hat. They can be likened to children, and you would not expect a child to accept much responsibility, would you? Geminians can be a sore trial to their partners and many of them bring infidelity and financial problems into their marriages. There is no point in reprimanding this type for they will honestly not understand how it has all happened. Boredom, then, is the greatest threat to the Geminian marriage. They need to be kept on their toes, if they are to be kept at all.

ARIES March 21 — April 20

Impulse is the greatest danger to subjects of Aries. They jump into love one day and then out the next, both at great speed. Because of their conveniently short memories they rarely learn from past mistakes. Many born under this sign pass through several marriages before they begin to realize that they must be doing something wrong. If they could only slow down and think before making a commitment they would save themselves a great deal of trouble.

SAGITTARIUS November 23 — December 21

Marriage and Sagittarius could be likened to sausages and custard — incompatible. All Sagittarians possess a keen sense of freedom and to them it is invaluable, so it is not easy for anyone to persuade them into truly giving it up. The typical Sagittarian needs to constantly pit his/her wits against the opposite sex and, because of this characteristic, infidelity is a common cause for divorce — although it is unlikely that this type will truly understand the meaning of infidelity anyway. Fortunately, their undeniable charm means it is easy for them to get away with murder. Most of the time.